# A Moving Subject

# Focus Animation

*Series Editor:*

Giannalberto Bendazzi

**The Focus Animation Series** aims to provide unique, accessible content that may not otherwise be published. We allow researchers, academics, and professionals the ability to quickly publish high impact, current literature in the field of animation for a global audience.

This series is a fine complement to the existing, robust animation titles available through CRC Press/Focal Press.

**Series Editor Giannalberto Bendazzi**, currently an independent scholar, is a former Visiting Professor of History of Animation at the Nanyang Technological University in Singapore and a former professor at the Università degli Studi di Milano. We welcome any submissions to help grow the wonderful content we are striving to provide to the animation community: giannalbertobendazzi@gmail.com.

# A Moving Subject

Giannalberto Bendazzi

**CRC Press**
Taylor & Francis Group
Boca Raton  London  New York

CRC Press is an imprint of the
Taylor & Francis Group, an **informa** business

First edition published 2021
by CRC Press
6000 Broken Sound Parkway NW, Suite 300, Boca Raton, FL 33487-2742

and by CRC Press
2 Park Square, Milton Park, Abingdon, Oxon, OX14 4RN

© 2021 Taylor & Francis Group, LLC

CRC Press is an imprint of Taylor & Francis Group, LLC

CV 12.21.2020 1421

ISBN: 978-0-367-56185-7 (hbk)
ISBN: 978-0-367-56689-0 (pbk)
ISBN: 978-1-003-09897-3 (ebk)

*For Ilaria*

# Contents

# Author

A FORMER PROFESSOR AT THE Nanyang Technological University of Singapore and the Università degli Studi of Milan, Italian-born Giannalberto Bendazzi has thoroughly investigated the history of animation for more than forty years. A founding member of the Society for Animation Studies, he has authored or edited various classics in various languages and has lectured extensively on every continent. He received an honorary doctorate from Lisbon University in 2019. He is the editor of the Focus Animation series of books for CRC Press. He also is the author of the three-volume set *Animation - A World History* (CRC Press 2016).

# Introduction

THE READER WILL FIND diverse essays collected in this book, and I am confident that they will not view them as disparate. The same standpoint and the same love are actually at the base of historical research like the one on the first abstract colour experiments, of a theoretical effort at defining the medium, of a reasoning on early African animated films, and so on, from 1972 to today. In my long career in animation I have contributed a world history, a monograph on pioneer Quirino Cristiani, and an anthological monograph on master Alexandre Alexeieff. It seemed fair to me not to deprive the collected essays (otherwise unobtainable) to readers who value my work.

# CHAPTER 1

# The Italians Who Invented the Drawn-on-Film Technique*

T HE BROTHERS ARNALDO GINANNI Corradini (1890–1982) and Bruno Ginanni Corradini (1892–1976) were born in Ravenna, Italy, into an aristocratic (they were earls) and educated family. At a very early age, they started cultivating poetry, writing, and painting. They also took an active role in the debate between "Tradition" and "Modernism" that agitated the realms of literature, art, and music in Italy, from the turn of the century until the outbreak of World War I. Arnaldo mainly involved himself with painting, while Bruno focused more on literature.

After 1914, the brothers joined the Futurist movement, where they used pseudonyms, Arnaldo Ginna and Bruno Corra, to

---

* Originally published in *Animation Journal*, Tustin, California, Spring 1996. Updated version.

distinguish their separate identities. For convenience we will refer to them by their pseudonyms in this chapter, even though some statements were actually published under their true names.

Fascinated by the possible correspondence between sound and colour, in about 1909 the brothers created a "chromatic piano" whose keys corresponded to a parallel number of coloured light bulbs. Subsequently they carried out several experiments with what we now call direct painting on film, abstract cinema, or coloured abstract animation.

At first, they made a number of tests, including removing the projection shutter and projecting alternating frames of different colours to get an optical mixture of another colour. They then composed four films by painting directly on the surface of clear film strips to explore four different aspects of synaesthesia or correspondences between the arts. Lacking exact titles, the films can be called a "Thematic Development of a Harmony of Colours" based on a divisionist painting by Segantini (it was eighty metres long, or ten minutes running time); a "Study of Effects between Four Colours, Two Complementary Pairs"; a "Translation and Adaptation of Mendelssohn's Spring Song Intertwined with a Theme from a Chopin Waltz"; and a "Translation of Mallarmé's Poem 'Flowers' into Colours".[1] The longest of these films was more than 200 metres – around twelve minutes in projection. They subsequently "sketched" three more experiments on film strips (it is not clear whether they fully completed the films in a rough form or just made sample frames like a storyboard).

These three works explored abstract visual phenomena. One begins with a pure green screen, then a tiny red star appears in the middle, grows until the screen is all red, and then green spots burst out and reclaim the whole screen, making it all green again "for a whole minute". The second work develops a white and a yellow line moving over a solid blue background. The third shows seven cubes, each a colour of the rainbow, moving, layering, and warping against a black background. The last two films, again about eleven minutes in length, bear formal titles. *The Rainbow* is a "symphony" in which the spectrum of colours "throb", "bubble", "drown", and "explode" against a grey background. In *The Dance*, the dominant colours crimson, violet, and yellow continuously separate, unite, and "whirl upwards as the most agile pirouettes of spinning tops".

Scholars have often doubted the existence of these six (or maybe nine) films, especially because up to the present (and very likely forever) actual prints of the films have never been found. The only original source we can relate to is a chapter in a volume called *L'esilio di D'Annunzio e il "San Sebastiano" (D'Annunzio's Exile and the "Saint Sebastian")* edited by Bruno Corra and Emilio Settimelli and published in 1912 in Bologna by Libreria L. Beltrami. I will try to prove that this source is totally reliable, and thus that these films really existed, with all the theoretical and historical ramifications that this implies.

*D'Annunzio's Exile and the "Saint Sebastian"* is a peculiar volume, and its description is necessary to understand the significance and the assumptions of the particular chapter we will scrutinise. In fact, it is not a book in the strictest sense, but rather a "monograph" in a magazine, which Corra and Settimelli published after their literary weekly *A Defense of Art*, published in Florence for the two previous years, had failed. Their intention was to proceed, through this new format, with their line of thought that had been interrupted.

They also wanted to start a series of volumes/magazines with the collaboration of the members of their original artistic coterie (see the introduction "What Is This Publication?" pp. 7–9).[2] The language employed in the volume is journalistic, colloquial, and, at times, like that of an open letter. Corra and Settimelli are not compiling closed essays, but rather passionately pursuing a dialogue with an ideal reader that they feel close to and involved with. In Bruno Corra's chapter, "Chromatic Music", he describes in minute detail the experiments that he carried out together with his brother Arnaldo. He offers a vast array of technical details, describing both successes and failures of the various tests. At the end, he also addresses himself directly to anyone interested in these experiments, inviting them to write to him, offering him the chance to give more details.

Is this source reliable?

If it is reliable, what exactly are the correct dates for the films that it mentions?

The answer to the first question must be positive. Corra's essay presents the tone and language of a recent discovery, which he announces to friends and colleagues, inviting them all to follow this new and certain path. At one point in the essay, Corra even says where he keeps the films: in the drawer of the desk where he is writing. Furthermore, the text is supported by a variety of "technical" details that would be unknown except through direct, practical experience. Finally, he calls for other people to join in and share his experience – a call that no imposter would make, since they would run the risk of a competitor coming to inspect his studio and find out the truth – something particularly dangerous in the climate of personal and ideological conflicts such as existed at that time in Italy. Therefore, since Corra's text appears reliable, the films must have existed.

We can only deduce from reasoning when the films were made. Bruno Corra literally tells us that the first four films were painted "From last June to October". He then adds that the subsequent films were "done during the last few months". The book bears the date of 1912, without mentioning the month of publication. Does Corra refer, then, to the summer/autumn/winter of 1911 (with the book being published in the first three months of 1912)? Or does he mean the summer/autumn of 1912, with the book being published in December 1912?

Other passages from different chapters let us know that the two authors finished writing and assembling their texts during a winter; e.g., on page 14 Corra says "it has been snowing for two days" and on page 26 Corra refers to "one of my love affairs of two months ago – it was warmer then, it was autumn".

At least a few weeks would have been necessary for publication in that era. Each lead line would have been "composed" (picked up with tweezers and placed into a form), the pages would have been printed once for proofs (which had to be corrected), and eventually the pages would have been printed, folded, sewn, and bound – all by hand. It seems unlikely, then, that all this work could have been accomplished in the last days of December 1912 (which also contain family Christmas festivities). Even stronger evidence appears in the chapter "The Future Great Writer" (pp. 125–156). In the chapter, Settimelli reviews books by "young" writers, recently published, 126 titles "listed from October 1910 to December 1911, according to the *Bulletin of the National Library* in Florence" (p. 127). Since these reviews were openly biased, pertaining to the current ideological debate, it seems reasonable to assume that the author would want to express his opinion about the latest titles, so that his arguments would be relevant and up to date. Therefore, *L'esilio di D'Annunzio e il "San Sebastiano"* must have been published soon after December 1911. Otherwise, had it been December 1912, Settimelli would have selected books from summer and autumn 1912.

A final clinching piece of evidence for an early 1912 publication date comes from the chapter on Gabriele D'Annunzio, in which Corra refers to "Song for Tripoli" as something very recent (p. 36). These ten poems, inspired by the Italian–Turkish war for the conquest of Libya, were published in the leading daily newspaper *Corriere della Sera* between October 1911 and January 1912.

Thus, it seems most likely that Arnaldo Ginna and Bruno Corra produced their first four films ("Segantini", "Complementary Colours", "Mendelssohn", "Mallarmé") between June and October 1911, and their last two films, *The Rainbow* and *The Dance*, would have been finished a few months later. The brothers painted all these films directly on celluloid film strips (after the emulsion had been removed) using a special ink/paint used to tint photographs and slides.

The most important ramifications to arise from our study of Corra's text come from the dating of the films of Ginna and Corra.

We now know that an abstract cinema was born at almost the same time as abstract painting, since Wassily Kandinsky's first experiments with abstracting landscapes began in his water-colours around 1910. Therefore, we must overturn what has been considered common knowledge: that abstract cinema had started (around 1921) as an imitation and derivation of abstract painting – that painting, the "higher" form of art, had opened the way and inspired the "lower" art of cinema. In fact, abstract cinema was born from its own roots independent of painting. It pursued and accomplished the aspiration for a synaesthesia between sound and colour that had been prefigured in the eighteenth century by the French scientist Father Louis-Bertrand Castel (who built an ocular harpsichord) and carried on by various artists and scholars in the nineteenth and early twentieth centuries – perhaps the most famous example being the Russian composer Aleksandr Skriabin, whose "Prometheus" symphony, with colour projections written into the score, dates from 1910, the same year as Ginna and Corra's experiments with the chromatic piano and probably their first film tests.[3]

It is also important to remark that in Ginna and Corra's films we are dealing precisely with animation cinema, the same type that decades later would be produced by Len Lye and Norman McLaren. Corra tells us that he and his brother understood that the results could have been satisfying only if the film was divided into "bars", that is, by considering and painting the effect of the movement frame by frame. Finally, it is worth quoting the passage in which Corra tells us that he has tried to

> introduce into the sonata of colours something that could correspond to the accompaniment, which is so distinct in classical music. We prepared seven bulbs, each with one colour of the spectrum. By lighting one or

the other according to piano, while the symphony was playing on the screen, we should have had the creation of *colour environments*. [italics in original Italian]

While this experiment failed on technological grounds, in that the ambient colours bled and mixed with the colours projected on the screen, this experiment still anticipates various genres of modern-day performances, beginning with Jordan Belson's Vortex Concerts in the 1950s, and including "expanded cinema" and "light shows".

In terms of the concrete history of cinema, or rather of animation, the experiments of Ginna and Corra had no genuine influence. Screenings of their films seem to have remained confined to their home, and perhaps the only spectators were the filmmakers themselves. Nor is there any evidence that later filmmakers such as Ruttmann, Lye, or McLaren knew about Corra's article "Chromatic Music". Therefore, it is still fair to say, once again, that the filmmaker who actually inaugurated the "genre" of film-directly- painted-on-filmstock was the New Zealand artist Len Lye, whose *A Colour Box* (1935) has been widely viewed, debated, and imitated (especially by Norman McLaren, to whom we owe the vast diffusion of this technique, still present and vibrating to this day). But we still must not underestimate the almost prophetic importance held by the experiments of the Ginanni Corradini brothers, as well as the technical and theoretical remarks expressed by Bruno Corra in his writings.

For closer study, the text of Corra's 1912 chapter "Chromatic Music" is published in this book (see Chapter 2). It is interesting to note that in 1916 Ginna shot and edited the live-action experimental film *Vita Futurista* (Futurist Life), the only official film of the Futurist Movement. The "Chromatic Music" films were not his only cinematic achievement; however, *Vita Futurista* also seems lost, except for several still photos. The footnotes contain a number of books that are useful for further consideration of these two artists, concerning their participation in Futurism and their subsequent painting and literary careers.

## NOTES

1. The canvas by the Lombard painter Giovanni Segantini (1858–1899) is probably "Ebbrezza di sole" (Intoxicated by the sun), a girl lying in a field, painted several times around 1885, with dazzling spangles of colour in the meadow flowers – though it might also have been "Ragazza che fa la calza al sole" (Girl knitting in the sunlight, 1888), in which the girl sits in a field with farm animals, a fence and buildings behind her.

The moody, atmospheric Symbolist poem of Stéphane Mallarmé (1842–1898), in elegant rhymed French verse, gives many colour and action cues:

### THE FLOWERS

From golden showers of the ancient skies,
On the first day, and the eternal snow of stars,
You once unfastened giant calyxes
For the young earth still innocent of scars:
Young gladioli with the necks of swans,
Laurels divine, of exiled souls the dream,
Vermilion as the modesty of dawns
Trod by the footsteps of the seraphim;
The hyacinth, the myrtle gleaming bright,
And, like the flesh of woman, the cruel rose,
Hérodiade blooming in the garden light,
She that from wild and radiant blood arose!
And made the sobbing whiteness of the lily
That skims a sea of sighs, and as it wends
Through the blue incense of horizons, palely
Toward the weeping moon in dreams ascends!
Hosanna on the lute and in the censers,
Lady, and of our purgatorial groves!
Through heavenly evenings let the echoes answer,
Sparkling haloes, glances of rapturous love!
Mother, who in your strong and righteous bosom,
Formed calyxes balancing the future flask,
Capacious flowers with the deadly balsam
For the weary poet withering on the husk.

*(Translation by Henry Weinfield)*

2. The Table of Contents includes: (1) "La dedica al … Silenzio" (Dedication to … Silence), anonymous, but by both authors; (2) "Che cosa è questa pubblicazione" (What Is This Publication?), anonymous, but by both authors; (3) "Il pastore, il gregge e la zampogna" (The Shepherd, the Flock and the Bagpipe), by Bruno

Ginanni Corradini; (4) "L'esilio di D'Annunzio e il *San Sebastiano*" (The Exile of Gabriele D'Annunzio and *Saint Sebastian*), by Emilio Settimelli; (5) "*La Difesa dell'Arte* e il suo cenacolo" (*The Defense of Art* and its coterie), by Emilio Settimelli; (6) "*Chantecler*-interpretazione lirica" (Chanticleer-Lyrical Interpretation), by Bruno Ginanni Corradini; "Il futuro grande scrittore" (The Future Great Writer), by Emilio Settimelli; "Musica cromatica" (Chromatic Music), by Bruno Ginanni Corradini; (9) "Per un giudizio della *Difesa dell'Arte*" (For a Judgement of *In Defense of Art*), anonymous, but by both authors. These are, in part, literary controversies: in favour of Carducci, against D'Annunzio and the cultural establishment, while, on the other hand, espousing a radical modernist renewal with calls for proposals and new texts. The themes continue to be those that were typical of the literary magazines at the beginning of the twentieth century in Italy, promoted by very young elites of intellectuals: criticisms and praises, battles between cultural coteries, attacks against the "Old", aggressive displays of new proposals.

3. On the origins of Ginna and Corra's colour experimentation in ideal, mystical philosophy, Giovanni Lista wrote:

> The cultural choices of romantic symbolism dominate these experiments. The poetry that is applied in painting follows the method enunciated by Rudolf Steiner, who proposes that the weakness of sensory data be overcome in order to directly reach the screen of the consciousness' condensation … The so-called Occult [hidden] Sciences (theosophy, spiritualism, metaphysics, etc.) constitute the prime component in the cultural background of Ginna … The second component is to be found in the Wagnerian and proto-expressionist culture. The abstract short films confirm in this sense what I wrote a few years back in reference to Ricciotto Canudo: All the early theoreticians and experimenters of cinema as an art have been Wagnerians, for they identified within the filmic image the fluidity and immateriality of music. ("Ginna e il Cinema Futurista" [Ginna and Futurist Cinema], *Il Lettore di Provincia* [Longo, Ravenna, September 1987], 17–28)

There is no evidence that the abstract films of Ginna and Corra were ever shown in public, not even during the many Futurist manifestations of the following years when the brothers became active members of the movement. Indeed, their kind of experiment with pure abstraction clashed with the official Futurist ideology advocated and rigidly applied, especially by Umberto Boccioni, who wanted the Futurist artists to represent motion but only through static tableaux. The *Manifesto Tecnico della Pittura Futurista* (Technical Manifesto of Futurist Painting), signed by Boccioni, Carrà, Russolo, Balla, and Severini, published 11 April 1910, says, "We want the dynamic sensation manifested as such … Because of the persistence of images on the retina, things in motion multiply, deform chasing one another as vibrations in space they cross. So, a running horse does not have four legs: it has 20 legs".

# CHAPTER 2

# Chromatic Music by Bruno Ginanni Corradini (1912)*†

I ONLY WANT TO SET forth some facts. Nothing else. So, don't expect any attempt at elegance in my writing.

Should I succeed in making myself clearly understood, then I shall have achieved my purpose. I am writing this essay only to prepare the audience that will devote itself to fully appreciating and calmly judging the symphonies of colour which we will perform, I hope quite soon, before crowds in theatres. I wrote "we", meaning my brother and me, for it is only thanks to my brother, who is an accomplished painter, that the practical translation of this art vision (to which I can only offer my theoretical and intuitive contribution) can be made possible.

---

* Originally published in *Animation Journal*, Tustin, California, Spring 1995. Updated version.

† First published in Italian as "Musica cromatica", a segment of *L'esilio di D'Annunzio e il "San Sebastiano"*, Bologna, Italy: Beltrami, 1912.

At the moment, the art of colours that is being practised can only be explained through an analogy with painting. The painting is a "medley" of colours that are situated in such reciprocal patterns as to represent an idea. (Please note that I have defined the art of painting as an art of colours; I am not taking into consideration the other lineage that derives from another art form, for I do not want to digress excessively.)

It is possible to create a new and more rudimentary painting art form, by applying to the canvas masses of colours arranged in a harmonious pattern one with another, so as to please the eye without them having to represent a specific image. This would correspond to what we call "harmony" in music, so we can call this "chromatic harmony". These two art forms, chromatic harmony and painting, are spatial. Yet music tells us that something completely different exists, i.e., the medley of sounds that follow one another in time, the motif, the theme. So, by analogy, the Art of Colours can create a temporal form of art that will be a medley of chromatic tones offered successively to the eye, a motif of colours, a chromatic theme.

Some examples will surely help: a flower bed, a children's kaleidoscope, women's fashionable dresses, the stained-glass windows of a church – these are all chromatic harmonies. The moiré patterns on an iridescent shot silk, some types of fireworks, meadows blowing in the wind, a kaleidoscope rotating continually and gradually, the sea – all these provide examples of chromatic motifs.

In his novel *Le Lys dans la vallée* (*Lily of the Valley*, 1835), Honoré de Balzac has described extensively the art of gathering flowers. The beauty of nature is made up of motifs and harmonies; just glance around and you will see a harmony, walk and you will witness a symphony.

Almost always, in nature, harmonies and symphonies are combined in colour and shape – for example, those storms that offer frightening and powerful symphonies of clouds. Walking through a crowd means plunging into a beautiful symphony of colours, shapes, sounds, of tactile and muscular feelings, of balances, etc.

The taste for colour, which appeared strongly for the first time in the paintings of the Venetian artists (Giorgione, Titian, Tintoretto, Veronese, Tiepolo) has gloriously established itself in all European paintings of these past years. This tendency to give the art elements – colours, forms, lines, sounds, words – an expressive meaning rather than a representative one, is seen not only in the domain of painting (through Expressionism and the taste for landscapes – forms that aim at the music of colours), but it is also to be found in literature (through Symbolism), in music (through the innovations of Strauss, Debussy, Dukas, Ravel), and in architecture (through the Art Nouveau, with its indefinite, undulating, misty styles). The chromatic harmony is most suitable when the artist is trying to create an environment, especially in decorative painting. Recall the latest decorative endeavours of Klimt. [Corradini discusses written theoretical sources and musical forms for two more pages, omitted here.] So, two years ago, after having established the theory of Chromatic Music in all its details, we decided to make a serious attempt at producing a music of colours. We started thinking about the equipment that probably did not exist and would have to be designed by us in order to perform our ideas. We tried new paths, mainly guided by our intuition, although the fear of making mistakes always brought us to rely on the physics of light and sound, through the works of Tyndall and many others. Naturally, we applied the laws of parallelism between the arts, which we had already determined. For two months, we each studied separately without telling each other our results. Then we compared, discussed and combined our observations together. We agreed on the idea (which we had already formed before our studies of the laws of physics) to stick with music, and to transpose the tempered musical scale precisely onto the field of colours.

On the other hand, we knew that the chromatic scale has only one octave, and that the eye, unlike the ear, does not possess a *resolving power* (although, as I think about it now, I have some reservations about that). Thus, it became clear to us that it was necessary to apply a subdivision of the solar spectrum, even though this would be artificial and arbitrary, since the effect derives mainly from the *relationship* among the colours that make an impression on the retina. So, for each colour, we chose four gradations at equal distances within their spectrum – four reds, four greens, four violets, etc. In this way we managed to lay out the seven colours in four octaves: the final violet of the first octave was followed by the first red of the second octave, and so forth. In order to translate all this into practical terms, naturally, we used a set of twenty-eight coloured electric bulbs that corresponded to the twenty-eight keys on our keyboard. Each bulb was surrounded by a conical reflector-shade. In our first experiments, we tried using the light directly, but later on, we placed a pane of frosted glass in front of each light. The keyboard was just like a regular piano keyboard (except three octaves shorter). If you played an octave, for instance, two colours blended, just as two simultaneous sounds blend on the piano.

When we tested this chromatic piano, the results were so good that we thought, at first, we had finally solved the problem. We played with chromatic combinations of all sorts, composed some sonatinas in colours – nocturnes in violet and mattinatas in green – and we "translated", with some necessary modifications, a Venetian Barcarole by Mendelssohn, a Rondo by Chopin, and a Sonata by Mozart. But eventually, after three months of experiments, we had to admit that with the limited means of this chromatic piano, no further progress was possible. We could obtain pleasing effects that nevertheless failed to totally capture and hold one's attention. We had only twenty-eight tones available, and the blending did not work well. The sources of light were not strong enough; if we used more powerful lights, then the intense heat would cause them to lose colour within a few days, and then we had to colour them again with the exact shade – an enormous waste of time. It was clear to us that in order to obtain those impressive orchestral effects that can convince crowds, we would have to use an amazingly intense light – that would be the only way to leave the restricted field of scientific experimentation and enter directly the realm of performance practice.

We thought about the movie camera since. With slight changes, this instrument would be capable of offering excellent results. As a source of high-intensity light, it gave the best we could want. Furthermore, it also allowed us to resolve the other problem with blending colours, since instead of needing hundreds of separate colours, we could take advantage of the persistence of vision process to mix several quick colours into any particular hue on the retina. All we needed was to have the component colours pass in front of the lens in less than one tenth of a second. In this way, with a simple cinematic apparatus, with small equipment, we could obtain the numerous and powerful effects of the great musical orchestras, the true chromatic symphony.

But this was all on a theoretical level. In reality, we bought a camera and several hundred metres of film. We then removed the emulsion from the film and painted on the clear film strip, trying out a few tests. As is often the case, what we planned to do partially worked out and partially failed. In order to obtain a harmonious, gradual and uniform pattern of chromatic themes, we removed the rotating shutter and the claw action, but unfortunately this caused the experiment to fail: instead of obtaining the wonderful harmony of blended colours that we expected, the result on screen was an incomprehensible chaos of colours. Only later did we understand why. Then we put back in place everything we had removed, and we decided to consider the film that was to be painted as being divided into bars. Each bar was of the same length as the space covered by four sprocket holes, which, at least on Pathé film, corresponds to one complete rotation of the shutter, one projected image. We painted another piece of film accordingly and tested it out in projection. The blending of colours (which was our primary concern) was very successful, but the overall effect was less satisfying. We had, however, already understood that not much could be expected in this sense until we could develop the skill – which can only come with years of experience – of mentally picturing the whole gradual development of a motif as it will be projected on the screen, even while it is being slowly laid down with a brush on the celluloid. Such skill involves the ability to mentally blend several colours into one, and, at the same time, break down one colour into its components.

At this point, when we felt our experiments were progressing positively and stably, we found it necessary to pause and concentrate on all possible improvements to the equipment.

The projector basically remained the same, except that instead of the arc lamp that we had used up until then, we installed another arc lamp with three times as much power. We then tried different types of screens: a simple white cloth, a white cloth drenched with glycerine, an aluminium foil surface, a cloth covered with a paste which gave almost phosphorescent reflections, an almost cubic tent of very thin gauze through which the beam of light could penetrate and should have produced the effect of a swarm of white smoke. But eventually we went back to the cloth which we simply stretched on a wall. We removed all the furniture, covered the whole room in white – walls, floors, and ceiling – and during all the performances we wore white clothes. Up to the present day, we have never obtained better results, and we have continued working in our white room, which turned out to be very functional.

The results of this period of experiments, which ran from last June to October, consists of four little reels of film, of which only one is longer than 200 metres; they are right here in my drawer, packed in their boxes, *labelled,* ready for the future museum (please forgive what may sound like arrogance, but is only a father's love for these dear children, which please me so much with their little mugs dirty from the rainbow, and with their little air of mystery). The first reel contains the thematic development of a harmony of colours, taken from one of Segantini's paintings – the one in which we see houses in the background and in the foreground a woman lying down in a meadow. The grass of the meadow, all intermixed with little flowers, is rendered through the pointillist technique with a bustling explosion of varied colours; the grass is alive, everything vibrates, seems covered with a breath of harmony, you can see the creative power of Spring materialise in the lively spurts of lights – this chromatic harmony so impressed us that we developed it thoroughly in 180 metres of film. The second reel is a study of the effects between four colours, two pairs of complementary ones: red/green and blue/yellow. The third reel is a translation and arrangement of Mendelssohn's "Spring Song" intertwined with a theme taken from a waltz by Chopin. The fourth reel, perhaps the most interesting, is a translation into colours of the famous, marvellous poem of Stéphane Mallarmé, "Flowers".

Meanwhile, our artistic tools were improved, but, as every artist knows, these tools still often betrayed us. Obviously, we could not paint with oils the way you can on canvas. At first, we tried alcohol-based paints that were easy to apply and would dry almost immediately – but they also lost their colour quickly.

Then we tried the liquid colours sold by Lafranc, which are used for tinting slides, and we obtained good results from them. We also tried aniline solutions, tested new formulas from a wide range of books, and attempted mixing together different kinds of colours. Still to this day, the best effects have been obtained by simply modifying and revising the colours meant for tinting slides; we are still researching in this direction, hoping to develop a colour that, compared to the existing ones, offers more intensity and transparency. We have not yet, for example, succeeded in obtaining quite intense and transparent gold and silver colours, which should produce very powerful sensations.

We wanted to introduce into the sonata of colours something that would correspond to the accompaniment, which is so distinct in classical music. We prepared seven bulbs, each with one colour of the spectrum, mounted on a base that could be carried around the room. By lighting one or the other according to plan, while the symphony was playing on the screen, we should have had the creation of *colour environments,* which, in order to accompany the general tuning of the themes that were developing, would in some way lead the spectator into a proximity of feeling. When we first tried it, however, the light from the bulbs dispersed with similar tones to the film projection, causing a change in the effect of the symphony, making it excessively uniform, and only occasionally creating some pleasantly bizarre chromatic medley. Now, I will repeat, we are preparing to carry out this experiment again under new conditions which, we hope, will allow us not only to solve this problem but also to gain new insight and thus allow us to obtain a wider variety of effect and more space to freely move about.

I have nothing else to say on this topic. We still have not found more powerful means of execution. It goes without saying, though, that we have no intention of stopping at this point. Before performing in front of an audience, however, we will need to attain a higher degree of formal refinement.

All that remains to be said concerns the work we have done these last months, during which we have slightly neglected the music of colours because we were waiting for a type of clear film that we had long sought in vain, but now the Lumiere company had promised to give us some. We also both focused some on our respective art forms of painting and literature.

Before describing the latest successful symphonies of colours (since, for the moment, nothing more can be done), I will try to give the reader an idea, albeit a vague one, of the effects of a medley of colours extended in time: I will show the reader a few sketches (that are right here in front of me) from a film we have been planning for a long time, one that will precede our public performances, and will be accompanied by suitable explanations. It will contain approximately fifteen extremely simple chromatic motifs, lasting about one minute each, each one separate from the next. These will help the audience see the legitimacy of chromatic music, understand how it works, and, eventually, put the spectator in a position to appreciate the symphonies of colour that will at first be simple and then become gradually more complex. I am now looking at three chromatic themes sketched on celluloid strips: the first is as simple as you can imagine, with only two complementary colours, red and green; at first the whole screen is green, then a little red star with six points appears in the middle, rotating and vibrating its points like tentacles; then the star enlarges, enlarges, enlarges until it occupies the whole screen, the whole screen is red; then unexpectedly across the whole illuminated surface appears a nervous outbreak of green points that enlarge, enlarge, enlarge until they devour all the red, until finally the whole screen is green, which lasts one minute. The second chromatic theme is in three colours: sky blue, white, and yellow. On a blue field, two lines, one yellow and the other white, move and bend toward each other; they separate, curl up, then approach each other undulating until they intertwine with each other. This is an example of a linear theme as well as a theme of colours. The third theme involves all seven colours of the solar spectrum in the shape of small cubes, which at the beginning are arranged in a horizontal line on the lower part of the screen, against a black background; they move in jerky little spasms, they unite in groups, they crash against each other, break to pieces that quickly fly back together again, they shrink and expand, they arrange themselves in horizontal rows and vertical columns, they enter inside each other, they warp, etc.

And now all that remains for me is to bring the reader up to date with our latest experiments. These are two films of about 200 metres. The first is *The Rainbow*, and the colours of the rainbow constitute the dominant theme, which appears from time to time in different forms, and always more intensely until eventually it explodes with dazzling violence. At the beginning the screen is grey, then bit by bit on this grey background manifests, like the lightest of agitations, iridescent throbbing that seems to climb from the depth of the grey, like bubbles in a spring that rise to the surface, burst and disappear. The whole symphony is based upon this contrasting effect between the cloudy grey of the background and the rainbow, clashing one against the other: the fight escalates, the colour spectrum drowning in ever blacker tornados which whirl from the back towards the foreground; the rainbow struggles, manages to wriggle free, gleams, then disappears again and returns more violently to attack the edges of the screen, until in an unexpected dusty collapse all the grey crumbles, and the rainbow triumphs in a whirl of pinwheels, which in their turn finally disappear, buried under an avalanche of colours.

The second film is *The Dance*. The dominant colours, crimson, violet, and yellow, continually reunite with each other, separate and whirl upwards as the most agile pirouettes of spinning tops.

I have finished. There is no need for me to continue writing, for I can only offer a very remote idea of the actual effects of the colours. Each person has to imagine it for himself.

All that can be done is to open the way, and I think I have accomplished this a little.

Is there anybody in Italy who wants to be seriously involved in these things? If so, please write to me, and I will be extremely glad to tell you everything (and it is a lot) I did not have a chance to write here – and that could make your own work easier.

# CHAPTER 3

# The First Italian Animated Feature Film and Its Producer*

HISTORIANS OF ITALIAN CINEMA have always ignored *La rosa di Bagdad* (1949), despite its many important claims. This original production is the first animated feature made in Italy. It can also be noted to be the first Italian colour feature-length film, appearing three years before the live-action feature *Totò a colori* (directed by Steno, using the Ferraniacolor process), which is generally cited by scholars in this regard.[1] Additionally, the film represents a significant transition between a very rudimentary protohistory of Italy's animated cinema and its true artistic and industrial birth.

---

* Originally published in *Animation Journal*, Tustin, California, Spring 1995. Updated version.

*La rosa* was directed by Anton Gino Domeneghini (Darfo, Brescia, 30 April 1897–Milan, 6 November 1966) – journalist, writer, entrepreneur, advertising agent. It is especially fitting to highlight the work of Domeneghini because he was probably the one and only producer-entrepreneur in the world of Italian animation: a man who could have been the right catalyst, the "Italian Disney" for the whole industry, had he had more luck.

The film's first public screening was at the Venice Film Festival in the summer of 1949, where it won the Grand Prix in the "Films for Youth" class. On the same occasion, the animated *I fratelli Dinamite* (*Dynamite Brothers*, 1949), by Nino Pagot, was shown in the "Fiction Film" category. It was then that the dispute began (never to end) over which should be considered the first animated feature – and the first colour feature (live action *or* animated) – made in Italy.[2] This essay addresses many of these issues. It is based on interviews and documents provided to the author by the following people: the late Angelo Bioletto, *La rosa*'s character designer; the late Libico Maraja, the film's background artist; the late Raffaella Domizio Domeneghini, the producer's widow; the late Fiorella Domeneghini, the producer's daughter; the late Guido Zamperoni, the film's chief animator; the late Gianfranco Barenghi and the late Luigi Landenna, two of the film's animators; and the late Walter Alberti, director of the Cineteca Italiana of Milan.

As a young man, after having fought with the rank of artillery lieutenant during World War I, Domeneghini took part in the Fiume enterprise, by the side of Gabriele D'Annunzio, the famous poet and adventurer, and returned with a permanently disabled leg and a medal of valour. Politically speaking, Domeneghini was a supporter of the Nationalist Association, which merged with the Fascist party in March 1923 (five months after the "March to Rome", which brought Benito Mussolini to power).[3]

Domeneghini was a loyal Fascist and also held some political appointment but, with characteristic contradiction, he used his position in the right-wing party for helping the poor. His contradictions went much further: he was also a Mason, which was not allowed of Fascists, and a faithful Catholic, which was not allowed of Masons.

Early in his career, Domeneghini was employed in the field of publishing. For three years, he was the chief editor of the daily *La provincia di Brescia* (*The Province of Brescia*). He then founded and edited the monthly *La rinascita* (*The Rebirth*) and the weekly *Il giornale del Garda* (*The Journal of Garda Lake Area*). For many years, he was also the Vittoriale press office chief, again under D'Annunzio's orders. In this position, through the Sonzogno publishing house, he published the *Italians' Vittoriale* volume.

In the advertising world, Domeneghini made his debut in 1927, by collaborating with the American agency Erwin Wasey & Co. In 1929, he founded IMA (an acronym for Idea – Method – Art), an advertising organisation that was of great importance between the 1930s and the 1960s, until its breakup after Domeneghini's death. To give some idea of IMA's importance, in Italy the company launched Coca-Cola, Christian Dior products, Coty perfumes, Bosch refrigerators, BP petrol, Gillette razor blades, Bulova watches, and Hoechst colours.

When World War II started (for Italy, it was on 10 June 1940), advertising in the country became virtually nonexistent.

Domeneghini wanted to keep his staff of artists and collaborators together, so he embarked – more or less on impulse – on the production of a feature film: *La rosa di Bagdad*. The film was based on his own story idea, which he constantly modified with the help of scriptwriters Ernesto D'Angelo and Lucio De Caro. The crew literally began from nothing, due to the fact that none of them had experience in the field; still, they threw themselves, body and soul, into the enterprise.

For the production, Domeneghini hired the stage designers of the Teatro alla Scala, Nicola Benois (who very soon retired) and Mario Zampini; the musician Riccardo Pick Mangiagalli; the animator Gustavo Petronio (one of the few working in Italy at the time);[4] the executive producer Federico Pedrocchi;[5] the caricaturist Angelo Bioletto; and the illustrator Libico Maraja. At its largest, his staff numbered forty-seven animators and assistant animators, twenty-five in-betweeners, forty-four inkers and painters, and five background artists, in addition to technicians, general workers, and administrative assistants.

In Italy, cinema was at that time a small but strong industrial force. In the year 1940, eighty-three (live-action) feature films were produced, and the output continued at about the same pace during the war, with the exception of 1944, when the country itself was a theatre of combat and film production decreased considerably. By 1949, when Domeneghini's film was eventually released, the industry's output was just a bit larger, consisting of ninety feature films.

Animation, on the other hand, was still in its infancy when Domeneghini undertook the production of *La rosa*. Many people had tried to make cartoon films, but generally the results were amateurish, and the filmmakers gave up after one or two unsuccessful shorts. The only lasting work was done by Luigi Liberio Pensuti, who had made a number of educational films in Rome since 1928; however, technically and stylistically, his work was of little importance.

It is worth noting that, in this era of dictatorship, cinema was not actually used as a means of propaganda: the openly "Fascist" films were three or four in twenty years. Italian films for children (actually, there were few of them; children's true heroes were America's Mickey Mouse, and Laurel and Hardy) and children's literature were less influenced by true Fascist values than by the rhetoric of contemporary education: love the country, love the family, be obedient, be a good student, and be a good Catholic. This was in its own way oppressive propaganda, but it was also the same kind of education that every other European nation was giving to its young citizens.

Due to the 1943 bombings over Milan, Domeneghini and his staff (together with their families) had to move to the little village of Bornato, near Brescia. Here the production went on in two big villas, nonstop until the group broke up at the end of the war. At that time, Domeneghini was arrested by the partisans because of his Fascist past, but after a few months he was declared innocent and released. After this incident, he began working again and eventually rebuilt IMA into one of the most important advertising agencies in Italy, as it once had been.

*La rosa* was almost finished during the war, except that it became necessary to reshoot the entire film in Great Britain. Two cameramen by the names of Pellizzari and Manerba were sent to Anson Dyer's Stratford Abbey Films at Stroud to shoot all the scenes with Technicolor equipment, which was not available in Italy at that time. The film had already been shot with the German Agfacolor process, which was easily available even during wartime to a country allied with Germany, but a disturbing green shade had ruined the whole work. The final dubbing was done in Rome in 1949.

The plot of the film is as follows: caliph Oman, a debonair and good-natured man, reigns over Bagdad. His ministers, Zirko, Tonko, and Zizzibè, are everywhere esteemed for their knowledge (though, in fact, they are often simple and funny creatures). An ongoing problem is finding a husband for the caliph's beautiful adolescent granddaughter, Zeila. This young beauty has a crystal-clear soprano voice, which she uses to gladden her grandfather and others, accompanied by a teenage musician, Amin. A messenger is sent to call together all the princes who may seek Zeila's hand in marriage, but the wicked sheik Giafar, helped by the diabolic wizard Burk, plots to be the only suitor. Against him fight the musician Amin, backed up by the magpie Kalinà and the three ministers; unfortunately, the latter very soon are forced to give up, since drinking from the fountain of youth turns them into babies. Amin manages to escape from Burk and to find, with the help of a good fairy, the lamp of Aladdin, whose genie defeats the wicked. At the end, goodness is rewarded, and Amin marries Zeila. The film respects the rules of fairy tale, with the struggle of Amin corresponding to a "rite of passage", in which the adolescent matures, grows and therefore can become first a husband and then a king.

Although based on *One Thousand and One Arabian Nights*, the setting of *La rosa* is in a Bagdad of pure fantasy. So pure is the fantasy that one can easily detect an Italian Roman Catholic point of view in the film's "message" and in the philosophy of its characters, even if everything is set in a country full of minarets and lead by a clearly Islamic caliph. The Roman Catholic religion is evident even iconically: Amin's mother has the features of a Madonna and the old beggar looks like a protecting saint.

The pacing of the action is uneven, and, because *La rosa* was dubbed after its footage was shot, the finished picture looks a bit technically outdated. Nonetheless, it has good qualities as far as the development of the plot, the quality of the drawings, and the skilfulness of the animation. Some sequences are memorable: the dance of the charmed snakes by Amin's flute, his air battle with Burk, Zeila singing at sunset in front of an applauding crowd (a scene reflecting the influence of Italian opera), and the final fireworks. The three sages have too much in common with the Seven Dwarfs of Disney or the *Turandot* ministers Ping, Pang, and Pong; and Zeila is psychologically even weaker than Snow White. The Magpie is however a nice character with great audience appeal, and Burk is among the most wicked of the "heavies" in animation history. His personality is minimalistically delineated through his appearance as a black spot.

Domeneghini's wish was to create a moral tale, in which children could find delight as well as a lesson about good behaviour. This goal he shared with the pedagogy of his time. Domeneghini preferred sentimental scenes rather than comedy and often disagreed with his artistically strongest collaborator, Bioletto, who had an excellent comic mind. The combination of their forces causes the film to become a strange (but pleasant) cocktail of dramatic action and comic entr'actes, merged with a third element: the very beautiful sceneries of Libico Maraja, who established the story's atmosphere both psychological and narrative.[6]

It is obvious that the strongest influence on the film came from Disney's *Snow White and the Seven Dwarfs* (1937), a print of which had admittedly been studied frame by frame at the editing machine. Princess Zeila is a stand-in for the Princess Snow White, and the Three Ministers have the same comic function as the Seven Dwarfs. There is also some influence by the Fleischer brothers, given the "rubbery" animation of some of the characters. It would nevertheless be a mistake to undermine the influence of the Italian popular theatre of glove marionettes and, above all, the Italian opera.

The influence of the latter is evident in the music provided by Riccardo Pick Mangiagalli,[7] a rival of Pietro Mascagni and Umberto Giordano; even the psychology of a character is often described in music, in the purest operatic tradition. It is also evident in the actions of the characters. *La rosa* is, without a doubt, a film of drawn actors, rather than drawings in movement (something Domeneghini and his crew had learned quickly from the Disney lesson); but the performance of these characters is not like that of the cinema or stage performance. Actions are "exaggerated", "openly expressed", even "delivered", exactly as tenors and sopranos do in the opera.

According to rooted rumours, the results of the film at the box office were mediocre, and in years to come the film was always labelled a flop. The blame was laid upon bad distribution by United Artists. In actuality, though the film's distribution may have been underdeveloped, the actual box office figures show the film was not a flop at all. In the 1949–1950 season, *La rosa* earned L. 247,500 (equivalent to 2019 US$142,177, using a 2019 exchange rate), much less than the highest earner of the year, the legendary (in Italy) *Catene* (*Chains*), directed by Raffaello Matarazzo and starring Amedeo Nazzari and Yvonne Sanson, which brought in L. 1,470,000 (US$844,449). On the other hand, *La rosa*'s earnings do compare to a number of other popular films, such as *Miss Italia*, with Gina Lollobrigida and Constance Dowling (L. 189,000 or US$108,572), and *La bellezza del diavolo* (*The Devil's*

*Beauty*), directed by René Clair and starring Gérard Philipe and Michel Simon (L. 178,200 or US$102,368). Keep in mind that the average price of a movie ticket in Italy at the time of *La rosa*'s release was about L. 95 or US$1.35.

As this evidence shows, *La rosa* actually was a good performer at the box office. What then caused the film to acquire such a bad reputation? Almost certainly, it was a miscalculation of profit and loss. During the war, production costs were high and Domeneghini had to ask for loans from friends and former customers of IMA (one of the most generous was Maurizio Heim Esquenas of Calze Fama, a stocking manufacturer). In return, Domeneghini promised to double the investor's money or even – characteristic of his flamboyant style – to triple it. Actually, the film failed to meet its economic potential and the investment balanced its costs without yielding the promised big profits.

Part of the problem was associated with international versions. *La rosa* was triumphantly released in London (its songs dubbed by a young Julie Andrews); it was also successfully distributed in Belgium and France; and in the Netherlands it even inspired the creation of a line of chocolates called Rosa di Bagdad. Still, dishonesty and unkept promises prevented the film from becoming truly profitable abroad.

Domeneghini's experience with filmmaking left an impression on him. In later years, he abandoned animated features, giving up on the idea of a religious animated feature with a realist style (as he preferred), *Il Presepe* (*The Crib*) or *È nato Gesù* (*Jesus Is Born*). Instead, he concentrated his efforts on his work as an advertising agent. Apart from some commercials, the only animation produced by Domeneghini in the following years was a short film, *La passeggiata* (*The Walk*), based on the poem of the same title by Gabriele D'Annunzio and the inventive sets of the painter Gerardo Carpanetti. Toward the end of his life, Domeneghini made plans for a new feature film, *L'isola felice* (*The Happy Island*), which was supposed to use the combined techniques of live action and animation, but these plans never coalesced.

The estrangement of Domeneghini from animation is witnessed (as it often happens) more by what he did not do than by what he did. It seems significant that he did not take part in the booming market for animated television commercials, which occurred when Italian television was opened up for advertising in 1957. Production in this field flourished during the last nine years of Domeneghini's life: a period during which he remained a powerful media man, still strong and full of plans, and always in a position to gather his former staff members together in a film-producing structure. His absence from this lucrative market seems to reflect an unfortunate, self-imposed distancing from the field of animation.

In the final analysis, it is true that *La rosa* had very little effect on the future of Italian animation; in fact, it seems that a great amount of potential was lost following its production. Two of the film's most talented contributors, Bioletto and Maraja, left the field, soon followed by other members of the crew who went on to work in graphics, comic strips, and illustration. In the years to come, publicist Gianfranco Barenghi was about the only member of the production team listed on the film's credits to continue working in the animation industry.

Stylistically, the film also seems to have had little impact, since no other animated features based on fairy tales were made in Italy.

Certainly, *La rosa* did not draw the attention of critics, even if the press reported quite a lot about Domeneghini's project. Discussions of the film generally consisted of banalities about the abstract concept of its tale, the abstract idea of films for youth, and the daring plan of a Italian man to compete with Disney. The highbrow critics (mainly essayists) did not take part in this discussion at all. They had no interest in animated films, works for children and teenagers, or anything outside the central political-aesthetic debate at that time, which centred on Neorealism and its possible end.

The presence of an authentic entrepreneur like Domeneghini could have been crucial in the development of the Italian animation industry. Instead, its development was controlled by filmmakers who became producers (such as Nino Pagot, Bruno Bozzetto, and Roberto Gavioli) or shrewd opportunists of the market (such as Ezio Gagliardo, for his Rome-based Corona Cinematografica). One cannot find the presence of authentic entrepreneurs who dared to embark on a risky enterprise, starting from nothing, and without giving up in the face of great difficulty. Domeneghini had been clever enough to understand that one had to profit from the war to carry on production. He also managed to turn on the machine of marketing, at that time practically unknown in Italy, turning *La rosa di Bagdad* into a book (published by Baldini & Castoldi, Milan; then by Mondadori, Milan), a line of children's composition books, and a comic book. What he lacked, compared with a figure like Walt Disney, was that uncommon craze for his own enterprise and the egocentrism: he coordinated a bunch of artists he liked and respected, holding them only loosely to his own ideas, while the "Wizard of Burbank" selected and company-trained a crew of artists who would conform to his own vision of art and storytelling.

Furthermore, he was disadvantaged by having a studio in Milan, since the whole of the Italian film industry was based in Rome, where the political power stayed. The structure of the Italian cinema industry, tied to government intervention, automatically marginalised any non-Roman productions.

As far as the history of Italian animated film is concerned, it seems that Domeneghini was the right man at the wrong time.

Both Domeneghini and the Pagot brothers were outsiders, and yet they were agile enough to precede the heavy industrial machine of the Italian cinema in the rush to colour – though theirs were one-shot exploits. Too few were their followers for the establishment of a real animation industry, too little was the market until television advertising boomed in the late 1950s.

Thus, apart from the films of Disney in America, the animated feature remained a rarity. Of course, there were the silhouettes of Lotte Reiniger (*Die Abenteuer des Prinzen Achmed* [*The Adventures of Prince Achmed*], 1926) and some puppet films (e.g., the Soviet *Novy Gulliver*, by Aleksandr Ptuško, 1935), but very few had preceded the Italians with cel- and colour-animated features: the Barcelonese with *Garbancito de la Mancha* (1945, directed by Arturo Moreno) and *Alegres Vacaciones* (*Merry Holidays*, 1948, directed by Moreno); the Danes with *Fyrtøjet* (*The Magic Lighter*, 1946, directed by Svend Methling,); the Soviets with *The Humpbacked Colt* (1947, directed by Aleksandra Snezhko-Blotskaya and Ivan Ivanov-Vano); and a few more. Countries with a solid cinematographic tradition and strong resources, like France, Great Britain, and Germany, would begin creating animated features in later years. In Italy, one must wait until 1965 to see a film like that: *West and Soda*, directed by Bruno Bozzetto. In the meantime, many things had changed.

## BACKGROUND: LIBICO MARAJA

Libico Maraja (Bellinzona, Switzerland, 15 April 1912–Montorfano, Como, 30 December 1983) was highly appreciated for his painting, drawing, and, above all, illustrating. His experience as a background artist for *La rosa di Bagdad* was his only foray into film, but it was nonetheless a distinguished and very important venture: as a matter of fact, one could say that with this work he became the forerunner of a group of artists (Giovanni Mulazzani, Giancarlo Cereda, and Antonio Dall'Osso, to name only a few) who were destined to provide benchmarks in the Italian animated film industry.

A good colourist, with an incisive line, Maraja gave bis best to *La rosa*. He was equally skillful in portraying fantastic as well as naturalistic environments, and created soft, elaborate settings of landscapes and palaces in an imaginary East, influenced by an amalgam of colonial postcards, the architecture of Eclecticism, Hollywood movies, and the legendary *Arabian Nights*.

Maraja also illustrated the book version of *La rosa,* which Domeneghini adapted from the film. In the book, one finds unusually volumetric illustrations of the environment and figures, as well as a great gestural expressiveness of characters, underlined by a distortion that (perhaps unexpectedly) arises from Maraja's experience working frame by frame in animation.

In fact, when he first worked at IMA, as an animator, he revealed himself to be among the most sensitive to the Disney philosophy of "personality animation". In her *History of Italian Illustration* (Bologna: Zanichelli, 1988), Paola Pallottino defines Maraja's work as a combination of "fantasy-humor" and "grotesque elements".

Most of the artist's energies were devoted to book illustration, working for publishers such as Baldini, Carroccio, D'Anna, Fabbri, Mondadori, and Rizzoli, to illustrate the works of such authors as Andersen, Carroll, Cervantes, Collodi, De Amicis, Dickens, Dumas, Grimm, La Fontaine, London, Manzoni, Homer, Perrault, Salgari, Shakespeare, Swift, Twain, Verne, and Wilde.

Maraja's paintings were featured in an exhibition at the Broletto Palace in Como, 1–14 October 1982. In the exhibition's catalogue (Bologna: Zanichelli, 1988), Alberto Longatti writes:

> I have a feeling Maraja has always been, at all levels of his work, fundamentally an illustrator, in the literal sense of the word. That he has constantly "illustrated" one might say, a foreign entity, something outside himself; and therefore, that he consciously or not has avoided throwing himself directly onto the canvas. From this comes the particular configuration, and the original sense of mixing, in alternate periods, of realism and a gentle kind of expressionism, along with abstraction. In any case, what is more important for him is to paint: you can see that in the precision of execution and the refined completeness of the visual field, even in the most modest

pictures published in the illustrated volumes of novels for teenagers.

## BACKGROUND: ANGELO BIOLETTO

Angelo Bioletto (Turin, 30 September 1906–Milan, 25 December 1986) worked at IMA between 1942 and 1944, the three most decisive years in the creation of *La rosa di Bagdad*. Almost all the film's characters were created by Bioletto, and all accounts indicate that, after Domeneghini, he left the clearest and longest-lasting mark on the film. He taught his associates the need to "animate" – that is, to make the figures "play" and not just "move"; it was thanks to his constant perfectionism and drive that a multitude of novices working on the film acquired a professionalism and, in some cases, an authentic skill in the field of animation.

The artistic dyarchy of Domeneghini and Bioletto is itself probably responsible for the cohabitation of styles and plans that makes *La rosa* almost two films in one.

On the one hand, the producer/screenwriter/director (Domeneghini) intended to transpose on the screen a story with all the characteristics of a fairy tale: love, adventure, emotion; good against evil; and a final moral message based on the triumph of hope. His narrative grew out of assimilated traditions of storytelling as well as his own personal view of the world, which motivated Domeneghini's own behaviours at work and in society.

On the other hand, the artistic director (Bioletto) drew his great inspiration from journalistic caricature, the traditions of satire, the great comedy heritage of variety shows, and the cinema, to create a daring and merry film about the world of the intellectual (and quite extra-moral) laugh.

While it could be argued that both Domeneghini and Bioletto followed Disney's example, it is also true that one saw his Snow White side, while the other saw his Donald Duck side.

Bioletto was born into a wealthy family in Turin, shortly before his father went bankrupt, left the family and moved to South America. A self-taught caricaturist and graphic artist, Bioletto was already using his skills to earn a living when he was in his teens. For more than seven years, he drew a series of humorous cartoon columns (among them "Bioletto has seen" based on everyday life in town) for the daily newspaper *La Stampa*.

Bioletto became a national celebrity because of the radio program "The Four Musketeers", written by the humourists Angelo Nizza and Riccardo Morbelli. The program began on 18 October 1934, aired on Thursdays at 1:05 p.m., but soon was switched to Sundays, where it remained until 28 March 1937.

It has been said that the program was responsible for the sale of many radios; during its three years, ownership increased from 535,000 to more than 900,000. One day, Bioletto met Nizza at the entrance of the *La Stampa* headquarters (at the time, Nizza worked there as a reporter) and proposed to illustrate the program's characters for a competition hosted by its sponsor, the food manufacturer Perugina-Buitoni.

And so, the most popular picture-cards in Italy were born. One hundred were produced and enclosed into packages of chocolate and pasta. A person had to stick the cards into a picture-card album and, when 150 such books were collected, he or she won a Topolino car (which, at that time, cost L. 9,750 – ten times the annual salary of a good office worker). With fewer picture-card albums, a person could win many other prizes. Picture-card fever spread and the hunting of card number twenty, the elusive "Ferocious Saladin", became a true national pastime.

Eventually, the competition ended, World War II began, and Bioletto's contributions to *La Stampa* were stopped due to heavy interference by censors, who did not like the difficulties of the time to be printed so clearly in black and white. But the artist's fame and skill were very attractive to Domeneghini, who was always hunting for the best available persons on the market; Bioletto was offered a job immediately.

After his experience with *La rosa,* the Piedmontese artist no longer worked in animation. Instead, he tried his hand at comic strips a few times, then devoted himself completely to illustration for thirty years (until his death), creating plates for educational publishers.

## NOTES

1. It is worth also mentioning *Mater Dei* (1950) by Emilio Cordero, a barely distributed, barely known religious production.
2. Though they were launched at the same time, during the Venice Film Festival in 1949, the two films have different registration dates recorded in the Public Cinematographic Register by SIAE (Società italiana autori e editori). *I fratelli dinamite* was registered in 1947 with the number 672, while *La Rosa* was registered in 1949 with the number 799; however, SIAE's officials maintained that a given registration date does not imply that a film had been finished and ready to screen. For that reason, the 1949 date (of the first public screening) should be considered effective for both films.
3. The town of Fiume, in the Istria region (today Rijeka, Croatia) , was inhabited by Italians but, before the war, was the possession of the Austro-Hungarian Empire. The Versailles peace agreements did not award the town to Italy, and this outraged the public. D'Annunzio, at the head of a group of armed patriots, occupied the town, claiming it for Italy. This "coup de main" caused quite a heroic stir among nationalists. In the big and complicated mosaic that was later to be Italian Fascism, the Nationalist sector always had the "heroic" role and looked at D'Annunzio as an inspiration. D'Annunzio never completely accepted Mussolini's dictatorship nor his plebeian style and secluded himself in a rich internal exile in his Garda lake villa, named "Il Vittoriale degli Italiani" ("The Monument to Italians' Victory").
4. According to the book *L'Italia di Cartone,* by Piero Zanotto and Fiorello Zangrando (Padova: Liviana, 1972; a scarcely reliable source), Petronio was born in Trieste in 1889; in that case, he would have been fifty-three years old while preparing the movie. But, according to testimonies, he looked old at that time. He had heart disease and had to give up the production due to poor health.
5. Federico Pedrocchi (Buenos Aires, 1 May 1907–Milan, 20 January 1945), a scriptwriter and drawing artist, was one of the founders of the Italian comic strip industry. He was an editorial manager at Mondadori's in 1938, fought in the war between 1941 and 1943, and then – after working at IMA – became the editor of the Il Carroccio publishing house.
6. The animator, comic strip artist, and painter Guido Zamperoni, a key figure on Domeneghini's staff, revealed an odd detail during a conversation with this writer in January 1993: "I had a dear friend, former fellow boy scout, Nino Pagot, a good drawer. Domeneghini and I both thought to appeal to him, since he already had some experience with a cartoon movie and knew the basics of the business. But Pagot was not willing to join IMA, as he loved his professional independence". Pagot actually directed the animated feature *I fratelli Dinamite.*

# CHAPTER 4

# Defining Animation*

## *A Proposal*

**"ART IS EVERYTHING THAT** Mankind calls art", wrote Dino Formaggio in the introduction of *L'arte come idea e come esperienza*,[1] "this is not – as some might think – a simple opening line, but rather, it might possibly be the only acceptable and verifiable definition of the concept of art". I will begin by anticipating the conclusions of this brief study to suggest that the definition of animation[2] be formulated by paraphrasing the approach of the Milanese academic, and maybe with an ulterior accent on the time element to which he dedicated the paragraphs following this affirmation. (He analysed visual art thoroughly and therefore it is understood that, if one wants to categorise, animation is a subfamily in the larger family of visual art.)

Consequently: "Animation is everything that people have called animation in the different historical periods".

---

* Originally published in Italian as "Definire l'animazione" in *ITINERA – Rivista di Filosofia e di Teoria delle Arti e della Letteratura*, Università degli studi di Milano, May 2004.

I have taken the liberty to update the original language because, as a historian, I find myself particularly aware of the rapid variations in word meanings resulting from changes in mentality and – above all – in technology, which have taken place over the years and which I have witnessed in part.

It is important to note that between about 1895 and 1910 the term *animated* was applied to things that today are called *live action*, which we often group in a distinctly different category. At that time, "animated photography" was the common term, and a little later the equally rudimental phrases *moving picture* or *motion picture* came into use. I prefer this term instead of animated films for reasons that will become clearer later on.

*Animated cartoon* became official only after the first book on the subject was published. After that,[3] a glance at theatre programs issued from 1925 to 1939 by the London Film Society (one of the first and most prestigious film clubs in the world) is enough to realise that in the first half of the last century the idea of animation did not extend to the abstract films of Ruttmann, Fischinger, or Richter. Their works were instead considered experimental and grouped with others that in our time are known as live-action avant-garde films. Furthermore, the word *animation* did not exist as a noun – it was only used as an adjective with the "cartoon": *animated cartoon* (as used previously).

Later, in 1949, in his influential and very much studied work *Der Film. Werden und Wesen einer neuen Kunst*,[4] the theorist Béla Balász separated the two concepts by writing about "absolute" and "abstract" films in chapter XIV and "animated drawings" along with optical effects in chapter XV.

As far as popular opinion is concerned, most of moviegoers and even some of the cinema scholars continued for decades to think of animated works as a movie "genre", like westerns, space operas, war pictures, and so on. Some still think this way.[5]

The noun *animation* began to be used by French specialists in the 1950s, when an international cultural movement was consolidated between Paris and Cannes that attributed a specific meaning to this form of art.

The movement also objected to the dominant interpretation of the term, both in aesthetic and economical terms, popular due to the works of Walt Disney starting in 1928 (with the short film *Steamboat Willie* starring Mickey Mouse) and even more so in 1937 (with the feature film *Snow White and the Seven Dwarfs*).

In 1960, in the lakefront city of Annecy in Savoy, the world's first "Festival International du film d'animation" was held.

This movement set the stage for the birth in 1962 of the Association international du film d'animation (ASIFA), a sort of United Nations for directors, producers, and researchers in the sector. The preamble of its statute gave the first official definition:

> [While live action cinema] proceeds towards a mechanical analysis, through photography, of occurrences similar to those that shall be presented on the screen, animation cinema creates the occurrences using instruments different from those used for automatic registration. In animated films, the occurrences take place for the first time on the screen.

The second statute was adopted in 1980. After eighteen years of viewing works produced with the most diverse forms of image manipulation, it became understood that the original definition was overly dependent on the traditional concept of animated drawings.

Another definition was selected, using a negative format: "Any cinematographic production that is not a simple recording of real life in 24 photograms per second is defined as animation". At the time of writing, even these words are losing their meaning with the advent of digital techniques that are erasing the very concepts of cinematography, photogram, and filming.

At this point, it is necessary to try to identify some tangible element, without however bringing ourselves to ask whether a *specific animation concept* exists (in the same way that decades ago, during the quest to attribute a notion of art to film making, people began asking if there was a *specific film concept*).

If we took this approach, we would risk turning many theorists' or artists' "poetics" into a categorical "aesthetic". We would have to take sides for everything, wanting to obtain a lowest common denominator of the case histories instead of getting to the theoretical level. Moreover, once again, we would risk exposing the words to the aging process that deteriorates meaning through the passing of time and historical events.

This task needs to be dealt with, though, in order to begin participating in that generalised feeling that leads animators to perceive certain films as *their own*. In other words (in reference to the definition stated at the beginning) we need to begin to understand which elements have caused people in different time periods to call certain things "animation".

First, I'll try to clear the field of the misunderstanding that animation is movie genre. A genre has a reason to exist inside a certain form of expression. For example, in prose literature, there are several genres: legal thrillers, adventure, romance, science fiction, etc. In painting, we have portraits, landscapes, still life, abstract, etc. And live action films can be classified, as already stated, as westerns, soap operas, war pictures, etc.

"Genre" is a difficult concept for many, but in extremely simple terms, it could merely be based on a deal between the manufacturer and the user. On the guarantee for the user, that is, that this specific product will satisfy some of his specific requests.

To clarify, if you want horses, wide open spaces and shootouts, choose a western. If you like to be scared, go for a horror film. Genres are known for being repetitive – and therefore reassuring. Quite the reverse, films by top-name directors are innovative by nature. (However, we should not deny it has happened several times that a creative director with a stronger influence or a stroke of luck made an important film defined within a genre.)

Getting back to the subject, if one loves animated thrillers (a genre) and finds himself watching a classic film, he will probably be disappointed. Those who love Disney musicals like *Beauty and the Beast* have a strong possibility of being confused by an abstract film. Bugs Bunny's pie-in-the-face antics clash with the humour of Eastern Europe of the Communist era.

Therefore, many genres exist within animation. This is a good starting point for introducing it not a genre or macro-genre, but as a separate style of filmmaking, a brother to live-action cinema.[6]

When filmmaking began, in the last two decades of the 1800s, the practical application was based on the principle of bombarding the spectator with a series of still frame slides. Cinematographers and projector technicians knew that when static images are presented in sequence at a velocity of over sixteen to eighteen frames per second, the human eye perceives them as a fluid image. With a series of very rapid stop-and-go techniques, the camera photographed the successive phases of the actions that took place before it. The projector used the same procedure to present the images to the public. That was the system utilised to "write the movement" ("cinematography" = *kinéma* + *graphéin* in Ancient Greek).

The crank on the movie projector was turned by hand, and so the operator had an almost physical relationship with the film and its sequences. It wasn't hard to understand that, once the projection speed became standard, several "effects" became possible in the filming phase. One of these "effects" consisted in taking photograms one by one (stop motion) instead of using continuous movement, and changing the position of the object during the pause that the filmmaker allowed between one frame and the next. During projection, the object seemed to come to life.

This "effect" allowed for the development of a language. Through the single photogram technique, it was possible to invent types of movement that don't exist naturally, and in that way conquer the fourth dimension (time) after the two dimensions of painting and the three of sculpture.

This is what we mean intimately by animation: not so much the attribution of motion but the attribution of a soul (or a personality) to objects, forms, or shapes (even abstract) that are otherwise lifeless.

The language of animation was historically connected to the entertainment industry in a wide sense. It was first channelled into the production/distribution/projection industry for public entertainment businesses (cinemas); then it went into television and then the internet. Of course, it is correct to use the terms animated film, animated cartoon, animated short film, animated feature, animated TV series, or animated genre film (comedy, horror, western, etc.).

A question arises, though. When it becomes possible to attribute a personality to otherwise inert things through the use of technologies different from traditional filmmaking, can those products also be called animation?

A famous example tells us that yes, they can. Between 1892 and 1900, the Frenchman Emile Reynaud showed his *Pantomimes Lumineuses* to a paying audience at the Musée Grévin. The production presented brief comedy skits of drawings that came to life and action thanks to an instrument (not a movie camera) that he had invented, the Théâtre Optique. Specialists in animation have never had any doubts about including Reynaud among the pioneers of their art.

The language of animation shares many characteristics with its close relative, live-action cinema. Let's look at two of these attributes: (1) its ability to give life to works of narrative and non-narrative natures, and (2) its audiovisual characteristics.

1. The psychological component of believability is hazy in animation, while in live action it is fundamental. In live action, the realness of the actors and settings and the public's ability to identify with the scene is crucial to the film's timing. The spectator has no doubts that the action on the screen takes the same amount of time it would in

real life for real events, and his involvement in the personal drama on the screen allows him to not get bored if there are cases of prolonged close-ups, monologues, or dialogues in or out of the field.[7] Narration is favoured. In a way, we could say that live action cinema is comparable to prose in literature.

With animation, the public has to deal with drawn or painted images, models, or digital images. In other words, things that are not real. Emotional identification is more difficult, even though over time it has become easier because younger generations grew up with this form of entertainment and the use of symbols is commonplace in everyday situations. Narration is not excluded, as we can see from the existence of a large number of long films, but it is more difficult because the concept is based on stylised film content that the spectator must accept and interiorise. There are many very short works in which elliptical and symbolic languages are dominant, and so there is a certain liking to poetry – literature in verse – which also includes longer works but is at its best in short form, allusive, full of analogies.

Let's go back to the assumption that the base of animation is the attribution of a soul (or a personality) to objects, forms, or shapes (even abstract) that are otherwise lifeless; in other words, that the base of animation is the creation of movements and the choreography of shapes.

If this was all there is to it, we could say that it is just a specialised section of kinetic fine art.

2. The other half of the question (especially the non-narrative aspect) lies in the soundtrack. It's not painting – it's music. The animation language is exquisitely audiovisual. In the opinion of this specialist operating inside the sector, it is the most audiovisual of audiovisual languages.

Animated forms, figures, and characters have always had a close connection with music and sound in general. Musicians that work with animation have experimented since the thirties with the most revolutionary techniques. Music and noises and voices and sound effects have almost always been included together in the soundtrack, and thought to be of equal importance by musicians, who often made headway in this particular field prior to and better than their counterparts in traditional music.

If there are doubts about the sound/vision synergy, we could try a simple experiment: show any short film from the Golden Age of Hollywood without the soundtrack (for example, an episode of *Tom and Jerry* or Wile E. Coyote and the Roadrunner). We would see that the work would lose its weight and meaning without the sound. If this is the case with mass production and industry, the elite works would be absolutely devastated: for example *Strojenie instrumentòw* (*Tuning the Instruments*, 2000) from the Polish director Jerzy Kucia, a film that intertwines sound and images in an inextricable way.

Given the aforementioned examples, it would be superficial to think that we have touched on all of the numerous nuances and feelings that make up the idea that each person working in this sector attributes to the matter at hand.

The outer margins, in particular, are always in movement. Should we consider (or not) the old adage, "If this scene can be filmed live, it isn't necessary to draw it"? Is time-lapse photography (the technique that allows us to watch a flower bloom in seconds) a category of animation or not? What about virtual reality (used in flight simulators for student pilots)? How should we define the numerous touch-up operations that post-production technology makes it possible to do on images in films like *Titanic* or *Lord of the Rings*? Where it is possible to animate in real time, like it is possible to act in real time, do we have animation or do we have a puppeteering art instead?

In essence, and I apologise for the intellectual gibberish, the conclusion that we have reached is this: we can explore the phenomena of this particular creative branch of art until we touch on a categorical quality, but without actually giving it a precise collocation. Now – to draw conclusions and get to the point – we need to recall the definition made in the opening: "Animation is everything that people have called animation in the different historical periods".

This is not tautological, as it could seem. It isn't because it refers to an element that is outside the realm of pure words. It refers to the attitudes maintained throughout the various time periods by specialists in the sector from all over the world – diverse in culture and political and social conditions, but in agreement in their opinions.

This tells us that a language called animation exists as an autonomous form of art, with its own role and space. This also tells us that animation has its own place in history, just like any other relevant human activity.

In addition, this definition has the virtue of blocking the temptation to do intellectual gymnastics while splitting hairs in hopes of grasping the profound essence of the concept.

Many years' worth of experience in the field, in addition to a lesser amount of time spent in the library, have convinced this author that definitions are necessary and useful, on the condition that they do not spark intricate debates. Pure discussion often hinders the comprehension of life and/or creative works.

This study should be therefore taken as a non-dogmatic preamble to the actual work of the human sciences specialist, which consists exactly in achieving that very comprehension.

## CITED FILMS

*Steamboat Willie* (Walt Disney, 1928).

*Snow White and The Seven Dwarfs* (David Hand, 1937).

*Beauty and the Beast* (Gary Trousdale and Kirk Wise, 1991).

*Tuning the Instruments* (*Strojenie instrumentòw*; Jerzy Kucia, 2000).

*Titanic* (James Cameron, 1997).

*Lord of the Rings* trilogy (Peter Jackson, 2001–2003).

## NOTES

1. Dino Formaggio, *L'arte come idea e come esperienza*. Milan: Mondadori 1981, p. 11.
2. I prefer this term instead of animated films for reasons that will become clearer later on.
3. E.G. Lutz, *Animated Cartoons: How They are Made, Their Origin and Development*. New York: Scribner's, 1920.
4. Béla Balász, *Der Film. Werden und Wesen einer neuen Kunst*. Wien: Globus, 1949.
5. On 11 September 2003, the American doctoral student Shana Heinricy wrote a message to the internet discussion group of the "Animation Journal List" to ask for clarification. She said that the professors advising her for her PhD (!) thesis were making her call animation a "film genre" and she voiced her doubts in this regard. The scholar Maureen Furniss, coordinator of the group, answered sarcastically that if animation is a genre then so is live-action cinema.
6. Here, in order to once and for all eliminate the clichés, I insist that though there is a rather substantial number of animated production destined for children, it would be a grave error to catalogue animation as an art form for children alone.
7. For an in-depth analysis of this concept, see Midhat Ajanovic, *Animacija i realizam*, Zagreb: Hrvatski filmski savez, 2004.

# CHAPTER 5

# African Cinema Animation*

I F THE TOPIC IS "African cinema animation", a question will most certainly be asked: What do we really know about it? Does anybody know anything about it? Amongst the forms of expression of the twentieth and twenty-first centuries, cinema animation is unanimously considered to be the most underestimated, the least explored, and the most misunderstood of all. Within this dispiriting framework, African cinema animation suffers the worst-case scenario. Let us have a look at the written sources: apart from some monographs on the film and theatre director William Kentridge (Republic of South Africa), the precious but thin collection of works by the Swiss Bruno Edera,[1] and the equally thin chapter on this topic in my world history of cinema animation,[2] what we non-African people know about this issue comes from a forty-eight-page booklet *Hommage au cinéma d'animation d'Afrique noire.*[3]

---

\* Originally published in English in the online journal *EnterText 4.1* in 2008. Translated from Italian by Emilia Ippolito with Paula Burnett.

Here is a significant quotation from Jean-Claude Matumweni Mwakala's essay *Aspects sociologiques du cinéma d'animation africain* (*Sociological Aspects of African Cinema Animation*) included in the aforementioned collection:

> As we all know, you need large investments to produce a film. The countries which have a prosperous and high quality film industry have invested large amounts of money in this sector. Africa has no cinema industry, and the existing investments are based on co-productions. The norm is therefore a lack of financial means; however, there are a couple of observations to make: for example, the waste of funds carried out by public authorities. The Ndaya International Foundation had obtained funds to finance the series *Kimboo* – which cost around twelve million French francs – together with France. It is known that film directors in Arab countries can count on policies of public financial support for their productions: it is the case in Tunisia, whose film productions have been made possible by the Ministry of Culture.

Matumweni Mwakala says that a lack of infrastructure, investment, and entrepreneurship are at the root of the troubles in African cinema animation. Is he right? If the animation films he takes as models are the approximately fifty episodes of the Franco-Ivory Coast series *Kimboo*, I would say yes, he is right.

Here is one more translated quotation, this from Benjamin Benimana's essay *L'esthétique du cinéma d'animation africain* (*The Aesthetics of African Cinema Animation*):

> The question we should ask ourselves is probably as follows: what kind of cartoons does the African audience watch? As you can guess, most African television channels broadcast cheap cartoons made in the Western countries, in India and especially in Japan.

Is he right? He probably is. However, why does he mention the "audience"? Does the "audience" exist only in relation to cartoons? Here is a quotation from Ngwarsungu Chiwengo's essay, *Le film d'animation africain vu de l'Amérique: le cas de Muana Mboka de Kibushi Ndjate Wooto (African Film Animation Seen From America: Muana Mboka by Kibushi Ndjate Wooto)*:

> *Muana Mboka* (a short film by Jean-Michel Kibushi Ndjate Wooto, Democratic Republic of Congo) is, in many respects, an important product. Since children in Africa and in other "third-world" countries are exposed to Western films which marginalise and erase black people from their environment, African cartoons play an important role in young people's education.

Is he right? He probably is. However, why does he mention "children" and "young people's education" without considering that cartoons can be regarded as for an audience which is not composed only of children?

I could add for the benefit of the viewer who is not up to date on the subject, that some productions existed in the past in Egypt (for example, films featuring the character Mish-Mish Effendi by the Frenkel Brothers; see Figure 5.1), and that a consistent production still exists these days; that the Maghreb region has also contributed to it extensively; and that other works have been produced in the past fifteen years, thanks to the method of co-production, to which Jean-Claude Matumweni Mwakala refers in his essay.

At this stage, however, I have to say that I will not express my opinion on this topic until we have eliminated some prejudices.

First, cinema animation is *not* a cinema for children. It can be and often is, but not in a different way from live-action films for children, pop music for children, and children's literature. Cinema animation is a cinema, twin brother to live action, with a specific history, a specific aesthetic, a specific market, etc.

FIGURE 5.1 Propaganda film made in the 1940s by the Frenkel Brothers. (Copyright Didier Frenkel. Source: Public domain.)

Second, the problem of viewers and television programmes affects not just African cinema animation but the whole world market (more precisely, the globalised market) of mass media. Separating them and analysing such problems as "African" or as typical of cinema animation means making a terrible mistake in the diagnosis.

Third, cinema animation does not necessarily need big investments, big infrastructures, or businesses. The example of Moustapha Alassane, pioneer of African animation and citizen of one of the poorest countries in the world, Niger, is meaningful in this respect. In 1962 the New York intellectual Dwight MacDonald published the book *Against the American Grain* (Random House), which included the essay "Masscult and Midcult". MacDonald was a contradictory and moody man, but he was ingenious. In this essay, which became a classic, he claimed that communication could be divided into three different kinds: mass culture (Masscult), middle-class culture (Midcult), and an elite culture (Highcult). For example, in literature, Masscult are

Barbara Cartland's novels and in animation, Japanese television series; in literature, Midcult are Stephen King's novels and in animation, Walt Disney films; in literature, Highcult is the Nobel Prize–winner Czesław Milosz's poetry, and in animation, the Russian Juri Norstein's short films, which are highly regarded and rewarded (at animation festivals).[4]

Sociologists and economists will not agree, since the state of the play is certainly more complex than this. However, forty years on, the division into three categories still serves for the examination of our topic, and those categories are even more exclusive.

First of all, if we question African cinema animation we need to know what animation we are talking about. The limited production of African animation will help us analyse it in detail. I will start with the Highcult and its pioneer, Moustapha Alassane. His films have been viewed and awarded prizes at various festivals all over the world; he himself has travelled a lot and has been a member of the jury at prestigious festivals (to my knowledge, at least at Annecy and Clermont-Ferrand). In spite of these facts, he can be considered as a *naïf* auteur. In the short 2001 film *Kokoa 2* (a remake of a film from 1985, about a chameleon fighter which changes its colour to red whenever it gets angry with its adversary; see Figure 5.2), he makes the same mistakes as to timing, script, and filming he had made in *Bon Voyage, Sim*, in 1966 – the first film of his I saw.

The fact is, Alassane has never studied animation. He has invented it. He has not adopted the conventions of timing, filming, scriptwriting, and editing established by Californian or Parisian professionals. He sticks to his own rules, which makes him an original animation director. Multi-cinema viewers, addicted to fast food, might not appreciate him.

However, his compatriots appreciate his films (by his own account). A *naïf* is not a particularly gifted troglodyte; it is a creator who does not want or is not able to accept academic codes, copies of reality, and colour theories. As for style, if the communicator has something interesting to say, we will certainly

FIGURE 5.2 *Kokoa 2* (Moustapha Alassane, Niger, 2001). (Courtesy: Copyright Moustapha Alassane.)

pay attention to him, even though he does not apply our rules. Moustapha Alassane presents us with his vision of Africa, expressed through very simple and cheap technical means, such as animated puppets, direct drawing on the film, and a few others; they are scarcely less simple or more expensive than sculpture and painting, traditional and popular arts which have existed for millennia. Every day animals are represented exactly the way they are (not in caricature): I'm thinking of the funny chameleon in *Kokoa*, or of the inflatable frogs which look like pompous and useless human heads of state in *Bon Voyage, Sim*.

A *naïf* is not a *Muna Mboka*, by the already-mentioned Jean-Michel Kibushi Ndjate Wooto, presents a similar case. The plot is almost negligible: a street boy, like many others in African cities, who lives by misdemeanours and theft, saves a minister's life (ironically, the Minister of Public Works), and is rewarded by him and envied by other people. A realistic (or, better, neo-realistic) film, a tough one, it denounces the African urban reality. Its colours are vivid and violent, its soundtrack noisy and "live", its characters paper-cut; this film is certainly not expensive. Kibushi Ndjate Wooto, unlike Alassane, is not a self-made director. He has studied cinema in Europe and knows the rules of cinema professionals; however, he often ignores them and uses a very personal timing, and clumsy frames and movements, aware that the topic is more important than the time he would need in order to mould the form.

Alassane and Kibushi express themselves through direct means (I repeat this word); they do not use filters. What are "filters"? Filters are big investments which may potentially generate even bigger profits; the large studios have to pay big salaries and be provided with good equipment and software; marketing and dumping strategies enable distributors to export television series cheaply: in a word, the industry. Moreover, the idea of entertainment meant only for children, or else political, ethnic, or educational propaganda – these are non-material filters but no less influential.

People who accept these filters also accept all their consequences. They will make films or television series which will be filtered, harmless, pre-digested, all the same, reassuring: films which will be based on universal stereotypes of movement, mimesis, narrative, characterisation, special effects (like the "Disney Dust", the sparkling stars which accompany any metamorphosis, noticeably in the series *Samba et Leuk*, directed in 1996 by France's Jean-Louis Bonpoint). At this stage, it is meaningless to complain against discrimination, conflicts between the world's North and South, whites versus blacks, colonisers versus colonised.

I do not agree with Benjamin Benimana when he comments on the aesthetics of African cinema animation (I am still translating from the aforementioned booklet):

> We need to remember three factors. The first is the "cultural virus" – the infiltration of Western cultural products into Africa. This situation does not help the

development of local products. What is worse: mass culture, independently of its origins and its producers' identity, is an industry of standardisation of expression and the emotional modes which carry its products along. Generally lacking specific moral values, this situation subtly destroys very ancient traditions, some of which have existed for millennia, filling them with superficial emotional cliches. The second factor is the major Disneyan aesthetic which has invaded schools and production in Europe and, at a later stage, in Africa. Uniformity has attacked originality and now it is essential to get rid of this artistic monolith. The third factor is that modern cinema animation has developed, and fortunately still is developing, a multiplicity of expressions linked to different artistic traditions, some of which show similar characteristics to the national schools. We think that a study of African cinema animation [...] should be based not on a search for aesthetic similarities with other products, but rather on meaningful differences, which can be used as evaluation criteria.

I disagree, since a few lines earlier he had consented to speak exclusively of "television viewers".

There are numerous examples of this production. *Kimboo* is a series of five-minute episodes in French, directed by Gilles Gay. The already-mentioned *Samba et Leuk* (1996) is a series of twenty-six-minute episodes in French, directed by Jean-Louis Bonpoint. In February 1998, Pierre Sauvalle – originally from Senegal, who studied at the Gobelins school in Paris – founded with Aida N'Diaye a company called Pictoons.

They acquired high technology, trained a lot of young professionals, and started producing television advertisements and soundtracks. Pictoons is the most important example of African animation meant for a global market, in open competition with European, American, and Asian productions. The first series,

*Kabongo le Griot* (*griot* means "storyteller"; it is a typical persona of African culture, which is based on storytelling), came out in 2000–2002. Its characters are a mix of international standard animation and, in the graphics, Fang or Dogon masks, typical of local cultural tradition (see Figure 5.3). There is also the mixed-techniques series (3D computer animation plus live action) *Grands Masques et les Junglos*, directed by Didier M. Aufort. This series is also in French. I do not know whether these series have been successful, but I must admit that they did not particularly impress me, as a viewer, with their aesthetic outcome.

Norman McLaren, great artist and friend of oppressed peoples, dreamed of animation as the language of developing countries. McLaren spent several years in China and India, teaching the basics of animation techniques to people who had only the most basic means at their disposal. We, the younger ones, also shared this dream with him.

FIGURE 5.3  Image from *Kabongo le Griot* series. (Copyright Pictoon Sarl. Courtesy: Pierre Sauvalle.)

Animation can in fact be quite cheap and technologically simple. In order to safeguard their personal inspiration and national cultural traditions, people from Angola, Liberia, Paraguay, Haiti, Bali, and Nepal can paint or draw their sketches on film and pay for it with their own savings, the same way they would create an oil or watercolour painting. If well done, their film will stay in the viewers' memory and cinema history books along with *Titanic* or *The Lord of the Rings*. It was a dream and it has not come true. However, never say never.

Since we are speaking about colonisers and colonised, please forgive this digression. In different contingent circumstances, I have witnessed two examples of colonisation during my life: Western colonisation of the West (the Franco-American, then only American, colonisation of Italy during the fifties and sixties) and Western-English colonisation of Australia.

The colonisation of my homeland has these days become homology. Italian cinema made by Italians for Italians (I mean "live" cinema, because of the inconsistency of animation products) has been limited to a few television comedians acting for the big screen.

The situation of the Aborigines was and still is different. They have been dispossessed of everything for centuries, and now the authorities offer them a sort of cultural compensation. I have witnessed a project of cultural re-enactment based on animation in Bourke, New South Wales. The aboriginal community, always tending towards visual means of expression, rapidly appropriated simple technological tools and started producing films. These films – this is the most important factor – refused to be "folk", and to propose traditional stereotypes. These films spoke of the Aborigines, their life, and their desires. A few years earlier, an institution called Aboriginal Nations had produced short films in which they tried to "set in motion" traditional aboriginal paintings and tell in this way some legends of the dreamtime. Easy exotics. It was a failure.

Going back to Africa, let me mention a talented white African animation director, Michel Ocelot, born in France and now living in Paris. He has avoided folk and exotic elements in his film animation *Kirikou et la sorcière* (*Kirikou and the Witch*).

In particular two big francophone countries, France and Canada, have invested time and money on animation co-productions, which are the best documented. Probably it is precisely these co-productions I am least interested in: they are not mulatto; they are half black, half white; indecisive as to whether they should be north or south of the Mediterranean, east or west of the Atlantic. *La femme mariée à trois hommes* (*The Wife of Three Men*) by Cilia Sawadogo, for example, is based on beautiful paper drawing and sombre colours. The story is derived from popular tradition in the Congo. However, in terms of style, you can find forty years of the National Film Board of Canada in it – it is a compromise. One more example could be *Succession* by Vincent Gles, also produced by the National Film Board of Canada: wonderful puppets, beautiful lights, great set design, and an African popular story. However, the author has accurately studied and applied the lesson of Jiri Trnka and the Czech school. One more compromise on the aesthetic level.

We should also discuss works produced by schools and universities, such as exercise or diploma films. I have extensive experience of this sort of production: in the last five years I have supervised so many such works. Everywhere, whether the authors were European, North American, Australian, Asian, or Third World students, I have found the same faults: blind trust in software, ignoring the fact that software is only a tool and not a thinking brain; blind and absolute trust in beautiful images, ignoring the fact that in a film, images should be moving; lack of interest in the diegesis (narrative evolution: the evolving plot, which should keep the viewer's attention high); and non-comprehension of the film as an audiovisual product, with a strong tendency to ask a composer friend for a couple of notes of soundtrack as a comment or to fill in the gaps.

I would say that the student-made films I have dealt with all had these faults, to different degrees. I had heard nothing but

good about Carlos Spivey, who is in California at UCLA and
Loyola Marymount University, but his works disappointed me.
*Mama Seed Tree*, which means to communicate the idea of the
continuation of life in the mother's womb as in Mother Earth's
womb, has weak images and the soundtrack is inadequate.
*Whisper* (fixed images opened up by software) and *The World Is
a Drum* are equally confusing.

So far we have spoken about black Africa. William Kentridge,
an anti-racist white South African auteur of about twenty film
animations, who refuses to identify his own work with the cartoon as such, is certainly the most important artistic and intellectual figure on the African continent. It is impossible to separate
him from the context in which he has operated and is still working at present. Born in Johannesburg in 1955, he has always been
politically and socially active, and won international acknowl-
edgment in the mid-nineties when apartheid finally came to an
end (1994). It would be wrong to look for overtly political mes-
sages in his film and graphic works (based on charcoal and very
few colours). Kentridge is a complex and at times cryptic creator,
who makes painful reference to the facts of his homeland, often
interiorising them like a poet, in other words leaving them to be
expressed by his protagonist, who will then become "everyman"
on earth. It is not by chance that his latest work is taken from a
highly interiorised novel, foreign to him, *La Coscienza di Zeno*
(*Zeno's Conscience*), by Italo Svevo (2002).

The first animated feature film from the continent produced
in 2003 in Zimbabwe, *The Legend of the Sky Kingdom*, is made by
white Africans – designer and producer Phil Cunningham and
director Roger Hawkins, both directing a multi-ethnic group
of artists. The film is about three children who escape from an
underground city where they are slaves, and go on to reach the
Sky Kingdom after a perilous and difficult journey. The technique, a variation on animated puppets, has been named "junk-
mation" since every character and scene was made by recycling
old objects, in fact, junk (see Figure 5.4). This was a respectful

FIGURE 5.4 *The Legend of the Sky Kingdom* (Roger Hawkins, Zimbabwe, 2003). (Copyright Sunrise Media/Sunrise Productions. Courtesy: Roger Hawkins.)

and affectionate tribute to this artistic craft typical of southern Africa, which at times reaches high levels of creativity and which was shown in an international exhibition in Bern, Switzerland, in 2000.

Then we have the Afro-Mediterranean cinema animation. Egypt, as we have already highlighted, had gained an international reputation in animation already by the thirties, when the brothers Herschel, Salomon and David Frenkel, directed *Nothing to Do*, with Mish-Mish Effendi as a protagonist; the film was followed by other sequels about the same protagonist. The films were not very well drawn, very badly animated, and with an even worse script design. Their model was not Walt Disney, rather the Fleischers or else Felix the Cat. As for the name Mish-Mish, it means "tomorrow with apricots", and we will translate it as "jam tomorrow": this was the answer given to the Frenkels whenever they asked for funding for their work. However, Mish-Mish and the Frenkels became so popular that they were able to start a successful advertising agency before the tensions between Egypt and Israel pushed them to emigrate to France in the fifties.

Film animation in Egypt saw a renaissance thanks to Ali Muhib and his brother Husam, who gave birth to the Film Animation Department within the national television channel which was inaugurated in 1960. In 1962 Ali Muhib directed *The White Line*, a film animation plus twenty-five-minute live action, which was a cross between a short musical and a documentary film. It was a lively and excellent film, which made fine use of the split-screen technique (unusual at that time), in a style reminiscent of Piet Mondrian. After eight years of work at the department, during which he trained many young colleagues, Ali Muhib successfully switched to advertising. In 1979 he directed the first Arab animation film series, *Mishgias Sawah*, composed of thirty episodes.

Mohammed Hassib (1937–2001) was one of Muhib's pupils; he separated from him in 1964 to devote himself to advertising, educational films, and live-action feature films. One more important person was Noshi Iskandar (Cairo, 1938), a well-known caricaturist. His first film was *One and Five* (1969), followed by the trilogy *Is it True, Abd and Al*, and *Question* (1969), inspired by the war between Israel and Palestine. In 1974 he directed *Where?* and *Room Number...*, a satire on bureaucracy; in 1975 he directed *Excellent*, a denunciation of corruption, and in 1980 *Narcissus*. One of his most faithful adherents was Radha Djubran (1945–1997), who authored the short animation films *Story of a Brat* (1985) and *The Lazy Sparrow* (1991).

Abdellaim Zaki (1939) wrote television soundtracks, live-action feature-film titles, and animation commercials for several Arab countries including Sudan, Jordan, Iraq, Kuwait, and Saudi Arabia (over one thousand), as well as didactic films. Ihab Shaker (Cairo, 1933), painter, caricaturist, illustrator, puppet master, was the most famous animation film director beyond the borders of his homeland. In 1968 he directed *The Flower and the Bottle* in Egypt, then moved to France, where he met Paul Grimault. With his help he directed *One, Two, Three* (1973), a surrealist film with a taste for anecdote, whose characters resemble amoebas. In 1993 he directed *Love Dance*.

Amongst the many Egyptian animation directors are two women. Mona Abou El Nasr has a very personal graphic style. Her *Survival* (1988), made during her stay at the Cal Art school in California, was very successful, along with the television series *Once Upon a Time* (1992). The second woman is Zeinab Zamzam, artist, musicologist, and psychologist, who directed *A Terra-cotta Dream* (1997), a combination of real images and plasticine animation sequences, and the excellent *Open Your Eyes* (2000), also based on the plasticine technique. Both are very refined pieces of work and make Zeinab Zamzam one of the most interesting artists of film animation in Mediterranean Africa.

In conclusion we can say that Egypt is the leading country in film animation in the Maghreb and Arab region at the beginning of the third millennium, and that its artists, technicians, and tools – both financially and technically – promise a great future. However, this country still remains, at present, prisoner of a self-imposed limitation: its products are destined only for Arab countries, and Egyptian directors at international festivals, the place where inspirational experiences are exchanged, are very rare.

I particularly appreciate the work of the Tunisian puppet animator Zouhaier Mahjoub, whose *The Guerbagies* was presented at the Annecy Festival a few decades ago. The government still supports its animation cinema – hopefully Zouhaier Mahjoub and his colleagues will be able to preserve a national culture in the right way.

The first Algerian animation film, *La fête de l'arbre* (*The Tree Party*) (1963), was produced by Mohamed Aram (Hussein Dey, 1934), only one year after the country became independent. Aram learnt animation techniques on his own; he trained his team and directed films in his spare time – he was mainly a scriptwriter. His first works were educational productions in black and white. *La fête de l'arbre* was an invitation to regrow the vegetation destroyed by napalm. *Ah, s'il savait lire* (*Ah, If Only He Could Read*) (1963) was intended to fight illiteracy, and *Microbes des poubelles* (*Litter Bugs*) (1964) deals with health problems caused by urban life. The large number of productions, over twenty between 1963 and 1999, did not help him solve his problems – a consequence of the lack of support from the cinema authorities in his country. Two of his helpers were Mohamed "Mad" Mazari and Menouar "Slim" Merabtene, directors and comic-strip designers. Mazari directed *Mariage* (*Wedding*) (1966), and Merabtene *Le Magicien* (*The Magician*), (1965). One more Algerian worth mentioning is Mohamed Toufik Lebcir, author of *Branches* (1991), based on the *Thousand and One Nights*, and *Atakor* (1993), the pilot episode of an eponymous series.

Now let us try and change our point of view. Let us completely abandon the notion of quality and consider the financial aspect only. Only rarely does history follow the rules of predictability, therefore I cannot see why African animation history should be any different. Here is a good example. South Korea was, until fifteen years ago, only a cheap-labour country. People who wanted to do film animation organised the creative phase and then left it to be made by the disciplined and cheap Koreans. These days, South Korea has become the third country in the world for producing television series, and short and long films, after the United States and Japan, and above France.

What will happen in fifteen years' time to the powerful Senegal, Egypt, and Republic of South Africa, where production companies aimed at television series are developing these days, or to the Ivory Coast and Zimbabwe? Will they have developed, as Jean-Claude Matumweni Mwakala says, "a prosperous and high quality cinematography, investing in this sector"? Will they have a well-structured, aggressive, and competitive cinema animation industry on the globalised scene, like the South Korean one at present? And if the answer is positive, how will they behave towards the Masscult and Midcult (in MacDonaldian terms)? My answer, though with limited interest – I must admit that I believe more in auteurs than in series – is that only then will we be able to answer the frequent and indispensable question: What is typically African in African cinema animation?

A cowboy in the nineteenth or twentieth century, or else these days, was as exotic in Boston or Manhattan as in Berlin or Manila; however, the Western genre is "typically" American. A giant robot can be found only in toyshops in Tokyo; however, the space-work animation of Goldrake is "typically" Japanese. The mentality and behaviour of the district of Trastevere in Rome is not comprehensible to Italians from Udine and Cagliari; however, Alberto Sordi's or Nino Manfredi's comedy is "typically" Italian.

I mean that cinema and television naturally depend neither on folklore, nor on old or new national or local traditions; for example, nobody in Italy has ever been able to make a good film on the very Italian character of Pinocchio. Cinema and television create their own mythologies (they are autotrophic, in this respect). These mythologies become national brands.

We can therefore say that Highcult auteurs' film animation represents the African soul, but as it has been rewritten by those auteurs. It in fact represents only those auteurs. The only "typically" African feature in their films is the soundtrack, taken from an eternal music, everlasting languages, French and English accents which never had to be invented.

On the contrary, a commercial product which is supposed to challenge, on the global market, other homologous commercial products, this will be the banner of the entire continent or at least of the producing country. In order to achieve this goal, it will have to invent an unprecedented style, an unprecedented narrative, an unprecedented life vision, and stronger tools than its competitors to be appreciated by the viewers. That is what the Japanese have been doing since the sixties with their series. Such a benchmark will become one more commonplace, one of many, waiting for history to follow one of the many rules of unpredictability.

## NOTES

1. Bruno Edera, *A la découverte d'un cinéma méconnu: Le cinéma d'animation africain*, Annecy: Festival International du Cinema d'Animation, 1993.

2. Giannalberto Bendazzi, *Cartoons: One Hundred Years of Cinema Animation*, London and Bloomington: John Libbey/Indiana University Press, 1994, 1995, 1999.

3. *Homage to Black African Cinema Animation*, edited by Lomomba Emongo, Strasbourg: Studio Malembe Maa ASBL, a co-production with the Cine-Club de Wissembourg, 2001.

4. Please note that all this is about production and consumption of cultural products, not their *aesthetic value*. There are numerous horrible films made by the elite for the elite, and numerous pleasant television series made by American, Japanese, or Korean chain productions.

# CHAPTER 6

# Alexandre Alexeieff*

## Poems of Light and Shadow

$A$LEXANDRE ALEXEIEFF (ALEKSANDR ALEKSANDROVICH Alekseev) was born on 18 April 1901 in Kazan, in Czarist Russia. He was the third and last child of Maria Polidorova, a headmistress, and Aleksandr Alekseev, an officer in the imperial navy. Aleksandr's brothers' names were Nikolay and Vladimir. One year later, Aleksandr Alekseev Sr. accepted the post of naval attaché at the Russian embassy in Constantinople (at that time capital of the Ottoman Empire and now known as Istanbul), and his family moved with him to the shores of the Bosphorus. Constantinople was a happy time for the boy, as he enjoyed the best emotional and material conditions that anyone could wish for. It came to a tragic end in 1906, when his father died in strange circumstances, in all likelihood murdered, in Baden Baden (Germany) while on a diplomatic mission. The family had to return to Russia and cope with a difficult existence in Saint Petersburg.

---

* Originally published in Catalonian, Castilian, and English as *Alexandre Alexeieff – Poemes de llum i ombra*, catalogue of the Sitges 03 festival, Sitges (Spain), 2003.

Though this initial chapter of the artist's life might seem a mere simple melodramatic anecdote, it is of decisive importance in understanding his future inspiration. That interrupted bliss gave rise to a perennial *forma mentis*, sowing in him the need to cling to the moment, to conserve the taste of every joy experienced, and cemented a nostalgic character.

In those days, Saint Petersburg was brimming with writers, painters, musicians, scientists, and thinkers; its theatre scene was buzzing, its elegant life shone. However, Alexandre Alexeieff barely got a whiff of what his new city had to offer. His time was given over to reading and to studying, to training, and to drawing in the Cadet Academy where his position as an officer's son entitled him to a place. Once again, an event in the early years of his life was to leave an indelible mark on the artist's career: his drawing master at the cadet school influenced him categorically by letting pupils explore their potential for fantasy, far beyond the constraints of traditional academic copies from nature. From now on, Alexeieff would never use models except on one occasion, when he turned to his wife Claire for help, using her face to illustrate Malraux's *La condition humaine*.

In 1914, Russia, allied with France and Great Britain, went to war with Germany and the Austro-Hungarian Empire. It was the beginning of World War I, in which the Russian soldiers, facing a German army that was well equipped, well trained, and well officered, fell apart disastrously. The 1917 Revolution put an end to Czarism and set off a civil war that was to last for three years.

In the most chaotic situation imaginable, those 16-year-old cadets were caught between the orders from their superiors and their desire to conduct themselves like self-sufficient adults, between the dizzying hopes of a radical reconstruction of society and humanity; and the daily horrors of the killings, the robberies, the violence.

One group of them was sent deep into Russia to await orders. Alexeieff was holed up in the town of Ufa, near to his mother's brother, Anatoly Polidorov, a socialist lawyer who successfully defended peasants and workers against the arrogance of the rich and powerful. His uncle asked him about his plans for the future, and Alexeieff replied that he wanted to be an engineer. "I thought you wanted to be an artist", quipped his uncle. Alexeieff, fired with revolutionary ideas, said that the country needed engineers to build a society that was new, prosperous, and advanced. "You disappoint me", concluded Anatoly Polidorov. Alexeieff reconsidered his future and took art classes for the rest of the time he was stationed in Ufa. Later he learned that his uncle had been killed by the Bolsheviks, who were somewhat less than accommodating when it came to rival ideas on the left. From that point on, Alexeieff steered well clear of ideologies and all that lurked behind them.

Three freezing months later, the cadets – those who were able to – reached Vladivostok, the furthermost tip of Eastern Siberia. They left on board a warship, but it was several months before they were told that the civil war was over. After a year of aimless drifting, Alexeieff chose France (whose language he had already mastered) as his new home. He still had a letter of introduction that the world-famous painter and illustrator Ivan Bilibin had given in Vladivostok. He landed at Cassis, near Marseilles, and settled in Paris in 1921.

## LES ANNÉES DE BOHÈME (THE BOHÈMIAN YEARS)

The set designer Serge Soudeikine (Sergey Sudeikin) read Bilibin's recommendation, and felt also impressed with favour by the novice's personality. In spite of Sudeikin's generous help and advice, the young artist's first year in the intellectual capital of the world was pretty hand to mouth, managing as he did to get only occasional work as a set designer. Things got better over time, and his new friends introduced him into Parisian circles. It was then and there that he met an actress with Georges Pitoëff's company, Alexandra Grinevsky, who he married in 1923 and with whom he had a daughter, Svetlana.

Closest among his new friends were the young surrealist poets, with whom Alexeieff shared a certain understanding about artistic creation: a maximum of spontaneity and a minimum of intellectual control over one's inspiration, to unblock the illogical and often unexplainable mind of the artist. It was one of these leading lights of surrealism, Philippe Soupault (1897–1990), who pointed the Russian immigrant in the direction of what would become one of his main activities: printmaking.

Soupault, who had put together a book on Guillaume Apollinaire, asked Alexeieff to illustrate it with a woodcut, to which he, a complete novice at xylography, agreed on the spot. With neither manuals nor masters available to him, and with only a few days to produce the image, Alexeieff invented the technique for himself, and on 10 December 1926 had in his hands the first of a long series of books enriched with his visual fantasies: *Guillaume Apollinaire*, published by Les Cahiers du Sud, Marseilles.

But it wasn't until a year and a half later, in June 1927, that the printmaking specialists would deal with the stylistic and technical expertise of an artist who at age twenty-six could already be considered a master. Nikolai Gogol's *Diary of a Madman*, published by Les Éditions de la Pléiade, included twenty-one illustrations in aquatint, a type of etching that makes it possible to get all the shades of grey between absolute black and white. This technique was well suited to Alexeieff's way of thinking, as opposed to the declamatory, exhibitionist, and frequently superficial attitude of the contemporary poets, painters, and musicians who populated the avant-garde. "They play the trumpet, while I play the violin", he used to say, unassumingly but lucidly.

## ILLUSTRATE OR CREATE

Among the aquatints that Alexeieff produced in his life, some were splendid, others good, none mediocre. Some of the very best were *The Fall of the House of Usher* (1929), *Colloquium of Monos and Una* (1929), *The Brothers Karamazov* (1929), *The Song of Prince Igor* (1950), *Hoffmann's Tales* (1960), and *The Works of Malraux* (1970).

Apart from a handful of commissioned etchings, he produced no "original" work, preferring to confine himself to pre-existing literary texts. In the field of *static* visual art, he was an illustrator more than a painter (to some extent, we could state that he was an illustrator even in the field of dynamic visual art, i.e., in animation; but we'll talk about films later). However, a question needs to be asked here: What is an illustrator? How does an illustrator work?

The attitudes of a man of images faced with the written word are innumerable. There are those who isolate a phrase and translate it into a drawing, those who take a suggestion and develop it according to their own inclination, those who identify with the story and those who simply rebel.

To Alexeieff, the concept of the illustration was that of free, independent reinterpretation of the literary text. To some extent, he always re-wrote in images what he was asked to illustrate, so that what the readers ended up with was, in the same book, a literary version and a visual version of the story. His masterpieces came thick and fast with the texts that he felt the strongest bonds with: Hoffmann, Poe, Dostoyevsky, and the extraordinary reinterpretation in images of Pasternak's *Doctor Zhivago* (1959), which enthralled even the novelist, who was able to see it shortly before dying.

In his work as an illustrator, he used those inspirational criteria that we have already mentioned: "surrealist" spontaneity, memory (Pasternak was astonished to find in these illustrations done by an immigrant who had left Russia as an adolescent everything that he'd seen as an adult during the civil war – "I can even smell the goods wagons", he declared), and another element dear to the surrealists because it was considered free of the conscious mind: dreams.

Alexeieff's illustrations are almost invariably a voyage into the unconscious, nourished by a reading of the book that he translates into images. At times, as in the case of *Hoffmann's tales*, the aquatints are rich (dense even) in symbols, analogies, and allusions that they become real visual poems to read, re-read, and mull over until they shed even their deepest meanings. This is the mental crossroad where the draughtsman fuses into an author in his own right, abandoning the secondary role of decorator of someone else's work. We shall soon see that as a cinematographic author Alexeieff was to latch onto the work of others, from Mussorgsky to Gogol, only for his independent inspiration to shine over and above theirs.

If we examine an engraving plate with a strong magnifying glass, we can easily appreciate the basic process of the creation of the image: where the plate is smooth, the ink doesn't get caught. This is why these areas stay blank during the printing phase. Where the plate is etched, it leaves a varying amount of tiny indentations, microscopic pinholes where the black ink is deposited. To the human eye, the black of the ink combines with the white of the paper, producing a grey that is lighter or darker according to the density of the holes, in other words, according to how much ink is retained. We need to remember this to understand how and why Alexeieff came to invent the pinscreen.

## CHERCHEZ LA FEMME (A WORTHY WOMAN IS THE CROWN OF HER HUSBAND)

Alexandre and Alexandra's marriage wasn't happy. Born out of a shared need for company more than for love, the young Alexeieff's age and artistic ambitions were at odds with the sedentary concept of family and fatherhood.

In 1930, Claire Parker was twenty-four. Born in Boston, Massachusetts, she was rich, good-looking, and emancipated but dissatisfied, so she left for Paris to join the group of Americans (Gertrude Stein, Ernest Hemingway, F. Scott Fitzgerald, Man Ray, etc.) irritated with the provincialism of their country, and keen to experience the intellectual stimulation of the international capital of culture. One day she found herself leafing through one of the books illustrated by Alexeieff and fell in love with his powerful, original art, realising that she had found her vocation. Shortly afterward she wrote to him asking for print-making lessons.

Their first meeting was so like the slushiest of romantic novels that one blushes to describe it in detail. Suffice to say that that instant saw the birth of a human passion and an artistic collaboration that was to prove itself invulnerable to the severe trials that private and external events were about to subject them to – beginning with World War II.

All the following auteur films (with the curious exception of *En passant*) would be credited to both of them. However, academics and critics have always referred to them as "Alexeieff's films". This attitude was partly a result of the innate sexism in our society and partly of the need to simplify matters for record keepers, who always prefer to identify one person as the object of their discourse;[1] but the decisive element for this option was a hefty dose of historical truth. For a start, Claire Parker always openly declared her role to be, artistically speaking, no more than that of catalyst – and cheerleader – to Alexandre Alexeieff's inspiration. As often happens, the gaps better prove to us what is real. Claire left us not one unpublished sketch, no technical note, and those who knew her never saw a pencil or brush in her hand or even a notebook. Her inspiration flew into his one; it added to his one; she completed him; she corrected him. Without her, he would have been a lesser filmmaker; without him, she wouldn't have been in motion pictures.

Alexandra, meanwhile, had come across a young artist of Hungarian origin, Etienne Raïk, and had made friends with him. We have no details about this relationship in its early stages, but in his old age, Alexeieff grumbled that, while he had been in a clinic getting over an intoxication caused by the acids used in his printmaking work, his wife devoted more time to Raïk than to him. Whatever the case, the two couples, now *crossed*, had a relationship of considerable harmony for many years, living opposite each other and working together on film commercials.

## THE PINSCREEN (ONE)

At the age of thirty, Alexandre Alexeieff felt deeply unfulfilled. Art had been his vocation, and after several ups and downs, it had made him famous, well paid, and well integrated with the world of friends and intellectuals who shared his interests and his passions. This goal, instead of seeming to him a much-coveted achievement, gave him the feeling that he'd reached the end of the road. Every new job from an editor, which would normally have been welcome, deep down meant repeating a technique, or a style, or a creative approach that was already well trodden. Limiting himself to a formula scared him. So, he started to think about cinema.

Between the end of World War I and the early 1930s, Paris bestowed upon the new invention of the film the rank of art. It chose the first great masters: the German "expressionists", the Russian Sergei Eisenstein, and, above all, Charlie Chaplin (to whom the critic, theoretician, and filmmaker Louis Delluc in 1921 devoted his first thematic book: *Charlot*). It hosted the most original avant-garde shorts invented by the painters Fernand Léger (*Le ballet mécanique*), Marcel Duchamp (*Anémic cinéma*), Man Ray (*Le Retour à la raison*), Salvador Dalí, and Luis Buñuel (*Un Chien andalou*), not to mention Francis Picabia, René Clair, Germaine Dulac, and some others.

> Cinema – said Alexeieff in the course of a long TV interview in 1971 – was certainly considered worthy of interest by my painter and writer friends. So, I said to myself: I will make films. Alone. I don't want a large team; I'm not looking for El Dorado. Under no circumstances must my films ever be a product. They must be works of art.

One day, the fledgling filmmaker asked his wife and daughter to go and buy him 3,000 pins. This purchase naturally turned into a small comic sketch when the surprised shop assistant asked for confirmation of the number of pins ordered. Alexeieff took possession of the pins at home, and the family patiently arranged them in geometric order on a painter's canvas coated with wax. Alexeieff spread out the pins here and there until he'd formed with them the shape of Svetlana's favourite toy, a doll called Baby Nicholas, and he finally allowed himself a smile of satisfaction. The test run had been positive; the pinscreen could work.

## THE PINSCREEN (TWO)

From my experience of more than thirty years of writing about Alexeieff, I can testify that the pinscreen and how it works is easy to understand when one sees it with one's own eyes, but less easy to grasp when one reads a description. I'll try to make myself clear.

The idea of the artist-inventor was to use a pinboard (though he preferred to call it a *screen*) upon which one arranges thousands of retractable pins, spread densely and set to an inclination of sixty degrees. He put a low-angle source of light at either end of the board. This way, each pin casts two shadows on the white surface, and the resulting mass of shadow makes the board completely dark. From this point on, all one has to do is to pull back certain groups of pins to reduce their shadows and make the corresponding area lighter. By pulling them out completely, any shadow vanishes, leaving just the illuminated part of the surface exposed. The artist was thus able to obtain a full range of greys in the creation of any shape. And this is where the animation comes in. Modifying the image manually and photographing it with a film camera at each new phase, the image comes to life.

It wasn't such a far-fetched idea as it might seem at first sight. Just think back to the principle of printing aquatints that we mentioned earlier on. Every small shadow cast over the surface of the boards equates with one of the tiny holes that absorb the black ink. Each white, lit up area corresponds to the bare (uninked) surface of the etched plate. In essence, Alexeieff managed to transfer the instrument that he already used for his static images into dynamic terms. He could now, definitively, make cinema out of animated prints.

## THE PINSCREEN (THREE)

"This will be the film that I wanted to make but never could", Alosha (this was Alexeieff's nickname) told Claire one day. "And why not?" she asked him. "Because I haven't got enough money, and for this job, you need a lot of money". Claire's American pragmatism could not countenance an unfulfilled aspiration. "I have a letter of credit. I can finance the making of a pinscreen and the production of the film".

Together they assembled their first pinscreen and patented it (in Claire's name as the banker), thinking not just about the film that Alosha had in mind, but also letting the instrument pay for itself by selling copies of it to animators all over Europe and the rest of the world. This latter scheme, to their great surprise, never happened. That device wasn't exactly what many creators were looking for. In fact, for a long time, it was only so for Alosha and Claire. It wasn't until 1972 that the National Film Board of Canada acquired a pinscreen. For decades the French-Canadians Jacques Drouin and Michèle Lemieux were to be the only other filmmakers who would use it regularly.

## UNE NUIT SUR LE MONT CHAUVE (A NIGHT ON BALD MOUNTAIN)

Russia was *far away* from Paris in 1931. In Moscow, political power was in the firm hands of Stalin, who was pitiless when it came to exiles. Many of them, gathered in various groups and ghettos (political, artistic, philosophical, religious, esoteric), spoke only Russian, excluded themselves from the France that was all around them, and chattering to each other about a return that they all knew was pure fiction. Alexandre Alexeieff frequented these groups for a while, at the start of his stay, and it was on one of those nights that he was dazzled by the piano playing of an old lady. He listened to her at first because she reminded him of his mother, also a pianist. But that evening the woman didn't play Chopin, as Maria Polidorova (Mrs. Alexeieff) used to do, but

*A Night on Bald Mountain*, a single-movement symphonic poem composed by Modest Mussorgsky in 1876 and arranged after his death by Nikolay Rimsky-Korsakov. The memory of that composition stuck in Alexeieff's mind, and he fantasised on it long and hard. When he decided that these gatherings of exiles were sterile and began to reconstruct his own internal Russia of the memory, choosing to live like a Frenchman among Frenchmen, *A Night on Bald Mountain* became the centrepiece around which all his nostalgia clustered.

For many days, in the darkness of his room, Alexeieff listened and listened to the recording made by the London Symphony Orchestra, conducted by Albert Coates, constantly fantasising around the piece. It was one of his ways to be a surrealist: the images surged involuntarily and dream-like from his subconscious, and he connected them later by analogy and without any rational thread to make them flow together.

He explained to Claire everything he wanted to put into the film, and she calculated the timing. It would work out as a piece of roughly forty-five minutes, which would need some trimming, as the music lasted a little over eight minutes. They set to it diligently, without any preparatory sketches that might spoil the spontaneity of the idea (the pinscreen itself, with the unpredictable but agreeably smooth touch of the steel pins, was also capable of suggesting improvisations to the artist-modeler), and at last, they were able to get down to the real work. In contrast to the tradition of animated cinema, the camera was positioned horizontally – like in shots of real images – with the pinscreen looming vertically in front of it. In a year and a half of continuous work, of reconstruction and corrections, Alexandre Alexeieff and Claire Parker made *A Night on Bald Mountain* and presented it to the public.

## FEW SEE IT, MANY PEOPLE TALK ABOUT IT

The short was screened for a couple of weeks in Paris and for a week in London. Today nobody would be bothered about an event that was so palpably irrelevant. But in the 1930s there was more respect for intelligence, and *A Night on Bald Mountain* was such a novelty of a film that it caught the attention of intellectuals and journalists. To a ripe old age, Alexeieff kept a thick pile of articles and reviews published when it was first shown. In *Le Temps*, the musicologist and theoretician Emile Vuillermoz wrote:

> Among the latest offerings from the technique of cinema, we have to make a special note of this animated print essay by Alexandre Alexeieff. A masterly adaptation for the screen of Mussorgsky's *A Night on Bald Mountain*. We find in the film a series of absolutely new effects, whose importance should be stressed. (...) These animated prints reject all elements of realism. They are not photographs. Everything here is composition and transposition. But this is not even the traced drawing normally associated with animation. What we have before us is a printing technique, a dictionary of subtle nuances, of a range of greys and of blacks, whose marks of light and shade wax and wane to infinity. Instead of playing with lines and angles, the artist uses the language of surfaces, of volumes and of figures with shifting reliefs. In terms of the relationship with the music, it can be said that rarely does a conductor accept the discipline of the score with so much fidelity. Some parts demonstrate just how much can be achieved in this field when one tries to avoid the separation of two artistic disciplines born to work together. When the spectral beings arranged in a circle hold hands then raise and drop their arms, or the moment when the music surges like a rocket and then falls like rain, what is achieved is a reinforcement of musical emotion of extremely rare quality. (...) This film marks a day to remember.

Stefan Priacel wrote in *Regards*:

Two admirable artists have just put together a short film of eight minutes' duration whose importance is such that I consider this to be a date to write in the history of cinema. The subject of these images matters little. Let's say that they are inspired by fantastic folklore of Ukraine, to which Alexandre Alexeieff and Claire Parker added their fantasies. There are hags and demons on horseback; there are witches' sabbaths that combine musicians and birds, horses and fireworks, landscapes that are calm one moment and stormy the next, in one oneiric vision. But the importance of the film lies not in the subject but in a change in procedure whose scope is such that it could be said to be to cinema what a beautiful painting is to a photograph.

In Britain, in the autumn 1934 issue of *Cine Quarterly*, the great filmmaker and producer John Grierson was beside himself with admiration:

The film, beyond its technical interest, is a triumph of fantasy. It's difficult to describe it, due to its startling nature. Try to image a Walpurgis Night in which animal tracks on the ground indicate the presence of spirits, where monsters and evil creatures appear, disappear and tumble about by pure magic, where scarecrows dance the fandango with their shadows on bare hillsides, where black and white horses race across the highest heavens, and skeletons that walk … Every art house cinema should show this film. It is the most astonishing, brilliant short that you will come across.

The distributors thought otherwise. They judged the film to be very hard for the general public to cope with, and the best they could come up with was to say that they would be willing to negotiate a contract provided they had a guaranteed production of at least six films a year, which was physically impossible. *A Night on Bald Mountain* started to make a bit of money thirty years later, when the US distributor and film specialist Cecile Starr put it on the American alternative circuit, on university campuses, and in associations passionate about art house cinema.

## LIFE IN ADVERTISING

In the Europe of the 1920s and 1930s (unlike in the USA) it was quite common to show commercials at cinemas. But the European mentality of those days considered that boasting about the qualities of a product displayed slightly poor taste, so the advertisers adopted the softer approach of *making friends* with the audience. In practice, the publicity film, which could be four or five minutes long, presented itself as a show entertainment – witty, fun, original – and suggested purchasing the product only at the end, after having ... forgiven the intrusion.

That meant that whoever had a creative mind could be given quite a lot of freedom so long as he was able to captivate the audience. Alexandre Alexeieff, Claire Parker, Alexandra Grinevsky, Etienne Raïk, and some other friends put their heads together and set off on this new path. Until the German invasion of France (1940) they all made a living from cinema commercials. On their return from their exile in the United States (1947), Alosha and Claire resumed that work and kept doing it for another ten years.

He didn't like advertising. It forced him to busy himself with things that had nothing to do with his inner world; it was just about selling objects. It put him in contact with clients whose myopia and arrogance he despised. For market reasons, moreover, what dominated was the use of colour, which he had always scorned, considering it a mere embellishment concerning the ideal work. And *that*, in his opinion, should be based on black and white, in other words, on the fundamental principles of yes and no, of love and hate, of good and evil, of life and death.

Despite everything, due to one of the many contradictions of the human soul, all his life he tirelessly defended the decision to devote himself to this work. He even declared that the painters of the Renaissance had no qualms about doing publicity for the Church, or court painters for their sovereigns, or the writers of *The Thousand and One Nights* for Arab merchants. Every retrospective organised in collaboration with him included his commercial films, of which he invariably showed himself proud.

These films have not aged well. They have lost any serious interest (with the partial exception of *La Belle au bois dormant*, 1935) and make patently clear the author's lack of intellectual interest. He rigorously avoids using the pinscreen, reserving it for more important occasions, and concentrates on small technical innovations to amuse himself and invent some motivation. At the risk of seeming too harsh, in my opinion Alexeieff's commercials tend towards kitsch and are best forgotten.

## AMERICA AND BACK

In 1940 Hitler's troops invaded France. The day before they marched into Paris Alosha, Claire, Alexandra, and Svetlana left the country and moved to the USA, where Claire managed to get each one of them an American passport in record time. Alosha and Claire settled in the New York suburb of Mount Vernon and began a humble but happy life. Photos from those years show them smiling and head over heels in love.

Work, however, was hard to get because New York was not yet the world's capital of art and galleries, nor did it possess the cultural and worldly finesse that it would develop by the end of the century. An animator could only draw cartoons, and an artist had to paint like Grant Wood or Edward Hopper if he wanted to sell his work.

It was Norman McLaren, who had seen *A Night on Bald Mountain* in London and was then working for the National Film Board of Canada, who sought out the couple and proposed a small project to them: illustrating a Quebec folk song, *En passant*, to include it in a series that the NFBC had just got going.

For this film, two and a half minutes long, a screen with 1,125,000 pins, the largest in the whole of the career of Alosha and Claire, was specially built. *En passant* (Passing by, 1943) turned out to be a minor anomaly in the artistic production of the two filmmakers. It was the only film not to be based on a Russian story, the only one credited exclusively to Alexeieff, the only one that portrayed an external situation (like an impressionist canvas, with touches of Monet) instead of the inner movements of the mind. It has some stunning moments, like the church that suddenly becomes transparent, revealing its interior, but at the end of the day it is a lesser work; and Alexeieff himself always considered it as such.

## ILLUSORY SOLIDS

The most abstract experimentation began in 1951, after their return to Paris. "Illusory" is a solid which, with long exposure time, is traced onto the cinema film by a moving source of light. The example that comes most easily to mind is the night-time photos of moving vehicles, published for many years in specialist magazines. The exposure is long, to get all the nocturnal light possible; the red tail lights and the white headlights don't register as points, rather as long luminous traces, which are "illusory" because they don't exist in reality.

Alexeieff decided to connect a tracing source (a chrome-plated metal sphere, which glowed when strongly illuminated) to a compound pendulum, whose oscillations were mathematically calculable and could, therefore, be predetermined. In this way, the different shapes that were traced in the air, one after the other, by the shining sphere could be predicted and controlled. Thus, it was possible to animate the illusory solids, those solids that were inexistent in reality. "What this is about – said the artist – is the second stage of the movement".

Though it was fascinating from a philosophical point of view, the nuts and bolts technique of illusory solids never merited more than a few seconds of film, normally used for suggestive special

effects in publicity work. In 1952 *Fumées*, for the Belgian ciga-
rette company Van Der Elst, won an award at the Venice Festival
for its contribution to visual innovation.

The year 1956 was also important for our cinematic history.
The prestigious Cannes Festival agreed to the request from various French filmmakers and critics, amongst them Alexeieff, Paul
Grimault, and André Martin, to devote a section to animation.
The *independent* (read: *non-Disney*) filmmakers had the chance
to meet and find out that they had interests and goals in common. In 1960 the first festival in the world specialising in animated cinema was inaugurated in Annecy (Haute Savoy, France).
Two years later saw the birth of Asifa (Association Internationale
du Film d'Animation), the United Nations of the sector. Behind
these initiatives invariably lay the discreet but determined will of
Alexandre Alexeieff.

## THE TWO GIANTS

In 1962 Orson Welles was involved with one of his many difficult
projects: *The Trial*, based on the Franz Kafka novel. He realised
that something was lacking, and he found it in Paris. Here is an
account of the event in his own words:

> (Peter Bogdanovich) – How did you manage to get the
> story illustrations for the prologue?
>
> (Orson Welles) – They're images made with pins,
> thousands of pins. I found these two old Russian (*sic*),
> completely crazy, cultivated, elegant, fascinating. It
> was Alexandre Alexeieff and Claire Parker, husband
> and wife. They sat down and stuck pins in a big board.
> The shadow of the pins made the chiaroscuro. They
> were two of the kindest and happiest people in the
> world. In my opinion, those images are extraordinarily
> beautiful.
>
> – Yes, they're really beautiful. How did you find them?

– I don't remember. I must have seen something on television or somewhere. They were working on a film; I think they'd been working on it for the last sixty years. I went to see them, and I persuaded them to interrupt their work for five months (not long, by their standards) and stick pins for me. They did it, and they did it superbly.

– Yes. It's one of the moments of the film that I like most.

– We should have made the whole film with pins! With no actors. A film without actors, what you and Alfred Hitchcock like![2]

As told by Claire Parker, the encounter had funnier touches: After a couple of calls from the producer, Orson Welles came to our studio. He started to look around everywhere, at all our equipment, getting more and more surprised. At first, he spoke to me in English; then he realized that Alosha also spoke the language well. From that moment he forgot my presence and addressed himself solely to him. It was entertaining to see these two creative giants trying to seduce each other, to win each other over. Eventually, they reached an agreement about how many images were needed, how much time was needed, about how much money was needed. Then, before leaving, Welles said to Alosha: "Could I come here when you're working? I'll just be sitting in a corner; I won't talk, I won't distract you. I'd like to see how you create the prints on the pinscreen". Alosha looked at him, and his voice became even more baritone: "One cannot refuse Orson Welles anything – he replied as if he were pronouncing a sentence – but I know my work would suffer"! So, he parted with a resigned smile, and we never saw him again. We found out, many months later, that he was very pleased with the work.

Orson Welles wasn't wrong in identifying the actors as the problem in his film. Indeed, *The Trial* has a fundamental defect: Anthony Perkins, too American, too

Hollywood, too short on nuances to cope with a role in which mystery has to turn into destiny and evil turn into life. His is a face in which one could probably read the neurosis of Freud but never, by a long way, the consummate darkness of Kafka. Many critics wrote that the prologue (based on another Kafka text, the short tale *The Judgement*) was better than the film itself. Alexeieff made it with fixed images, only slightly *enlivened*, darkened at some point in the developing process, while Welles's splendid voice narrates the story off screen.

Strange as it may seem, this one-off commissioned job turns out to us, as spectators, to be decidedly *alexeieffian*. The oneiric images of a mysterious large door, the enigmatic luck of a man trying to get through it, the atmosphere of fear that envelops the narration has much in common with *A Night on Bald Mountain*.

## THE NOSE

The film which, to give credit to Orson Welles, Alosha and Claire had been shooting "for sixty years", was a short adaptation of a short novel by Nikolai Gogol. It was ready in 1963, and it was called *Le Nez* (*The Nose*).

The original story was published in 1836. The plot seems like a dream (a nightmare of castration, we students of popular Freudianism would say these days) in which a Saint Petersburg barber, one 25th of March, finds a nose in his breakfast bread. The nose starts to lead its own life, talking and socialising. The owner, his face denuded, tries to regain the protuberance he has possessed since birth, until on 7 April, when everything returns to normality.

Although it was classed within the canon of fantasy literature that had existed since the birth of humankind, *The Nose* had such a pronounced touch of surrealism that it even to some extent upset Gogol himself. Devoting the final pages to a debate on the implausibility of the affair, he did so intelligently, ironically, self-satirically, but letting slip a sneaking uncertainty, ending with these words: "However you look at things, in all this there is something truly absurd. Nevertheless, whatever you say, in this world similar events happen; seldom, but they do happen".

The setting is as always Russian culture, and this time the starting point is a piece in prose instead of a musical composition, in some sense as if Alexeieff had decided to transfer his experience as a book illustrator to the screen. (It should not be forgotten that only very recently had he produced a huge number of images for *Doctor Zhivago*, choosing to work with the pinscreen instead of etching plates.) In this film, we find all the now-familiar themes: the surreal, nostalgia, Russia, the old days of the nineteenth century, the absurdity of things, the irrational breaking into everyday life, even comedy. And it's all mixed in a wonderful black-and-white dream, using a secret process that allows the author to make the images pulse just like the light pulses in his beloved city of the White Nights and of his adolescence.

## RETURN TO MUSSORGSKY

In 1972, for the first time, Alosha and Claire sent a film to compete at a festival (*The Nose* had been shown at Annecy but as a special screening). The result was bitter. The jury at the first Zagreb Festival decreed no recognition to the film by the two living legends of animation *d'auteur* and opted to award their Grand Prize to the Soviet *The Battle of Kershents*, directed nominally by the old Stalinist Iván Ivanov Vano and in practice by the unrestrained Yuri Norstein.

The work by the Parisian couple, *Tableaux d'une exposition* (*Pictures at an Exhibition*), was made up of three parts illustrating the three segments of the homonymous musical composition by Modest Mussorgsky dating from 1874.

Certainly, the jury made an error, given the film's indisputable artistic excellence. Yet in their defence it should be noted that there is no such thing as a jury that does not make mistakes.

Besides, given the extraordinary flowering of novelties coming from all the countries that attended in the early 1970s, this very personal, hermetic, black-and-white film made many, perhaps all of them, think that maybe Alexeieff was repeating himself sterilely.

As usually happens, the time has shown itself to be the best judge and the wisest critic. Removed from the emotion of its time, it reveals today all its exceptional poetic power, above all in the central piece entitled (oddly enough, in Italian) *Il vecchio castello (The Old Castle)*. This is a masterpiece of non-narrative animation, interweaved with well-honed visual hints and with unimaginable dynamic inventions. Surprising is the play of bidimensionality and tri-dimensionality created by the simultaneous use of two pinscreens, one of them rotating in front of one that's static. In a letter dated 19 December 1971, announcing the completion of the film, Alexandre Alexeieff told this writer: "I think that this film is as good as *A Night on Bald Mountain*, although it's very different. You need to see it at least twenty times before you can say that you know it well. That is something that good poetry requires too".

## THE MOON IS DOWN

With seventy years behind him, Alexeieff started to feel old. Claire was still smiling, displaying her natural cheerfulness and optimism, but the French Slav was showing signs of melancholy. In 1977 he mentioned that he was planning some last experiments and that he wanted to have a go at doing an animated version of *adagio* defined by the pace of its movements. He also said he was fascinated by the caressing movement of the leaves of a lime tree.

The experiments turned into the last film, *Trois thèmes (Three Themes*, also known as *Three Moods)*, based on three other pieces from Mussorgsky's *Pictures at an Exhibition*. In the first piece, we see an ox melting away in a Russian landscape, while in the second a string of images from *Pictures at an Exhibition*. The third offers a contrast between an obtuse giant stamping out coins and a brave little flying thing (and in whom we recognise Mussorgsky) buzzing around to try to get some attention.

Despite the fact that it has plenty of quality moments, this is a film made by an old man, by someone who has run out of steam. It is an attempt to summarise his artistic life and, more or less consciously, leave behind a spiritual testimonial. It is the work of a pessimist. The last *picture* in this *exhibition* shows us the heavy, rich Goldenberg producing money with his fists, while around him pants the tiny, anxious, creative Schmuyle. The former symbolises the power of the wealthy man, the latter the weakness of the artist. And the scales hang on the musical notes, ringing when the coins fall into his dish, but it changes its balance definitively when golden coins rain into the other.

"Alexeieff loved putting the moon in his films", confessed Claire Parker to the public in the soundtrack of *À coups d'épingles*[3] (*To the Sound of Pins*), a short 1959 documentary. In *Three Themes*, for the first time, we see no moon. Without giving too much importance to this element, which could have been accidental (yet, knowing Alexeieff's complex psychology, it doesn't seem likely), undoubtedly the missing moon is indicative of a farewell.

Claire Parker began to show the first symptoms of bone cancer in the spring of 1981, and after a great deal of suffering, she died in Paris on October 3 that year. Alexandre Alexeieff, beaten, survived her less than a year. He left us on the 9th of August 1982.

## NOTES

1. Normally, for example, one speaks of 8½ as "a masterpiece by Fellini", overlooking the fact that for the film he was able to use uniquely talented collaborators: the scriptwriter Ennio Flaiano, the set designer Piero Gherardi, the director of photography Gianni Di Venanzo, and the musician Nino Rota.
2. Quoted from the book *This Is Orson Welles*, by Peter Bogdanovich and Orson Welles, edited by Jonathan Rosenbaum, New York: Harper Collins, 1992.
3. Play on words: *un coup d'épingle* in French is "a small provocation".

# CHAPTER 7

# The First Reviews of *A Night on Bald Mountain**

*A* NIGHT ON BALD MOUNTAIN (*Une nuit sur le Mont Chauve*) was shown in Paris in 1933, with a critical success that had few equals for a short film of just over eight minutes. It had been made in eighteen months of hard work by Alexandre Alexeieff (Kazan, 1901–Paris, 1982) and by his partner Claire Parker (Boston, 1906–Paris, 1981), photographing frame by frame the images that were created utilising a tool invented by Alexeieff himself and called écran d'épingles (pinscreen).

It was a white, square board on which 500,000 retractable black pins were fixed. They were illuminated by two light sources placed on the two upper corners. Thanks to this lighting system, every single pin cast a shadow on the surface of the board, long in proportion to its output: in this way it was possible to obtain an absolute white (completely retracted pin) or a whole range of

---

* First published in *Immagine - Note di storia del cinema*, Nuova serie, nn. 38–39, Rome, 1997.

greys up to absolute black (pin completely escaped and shadow brought up to cover the adjacent pin). The principle, identical to that of the black dots on the engraver's plate, allowed Alexeieff and Parker to get animated etchings. The artistic quality was the same as the illustrations for quality books that Alexeieff had made in the 1920s, and for which he was already famous in the restricted milieu of the sector's specialists. The construction of the pinscreen, which he had envisioned since 1929, had been made possible thanks to the funds available to Claire Parker, who entered his life in 1930. In fact, the relative patent was deposited in her name, in recognition of the importance the funding had had.

*A Night on Bald Mountain* was based on the homonymous symphonic poem by Modest Mussorgsky. It was one of the most fascinating and vital proposals to solve the problem of the relationship between image and sound; as such it quickly became a cult film. Often it was more quoted than seen, also because of the difficult availability of copies. Many people confused it with the episode with the same title of Walt Disney's *Fantasia*, made seven years later.

This masterpiece of the first season of animation cinema predicted with extreme significance many of those characteristics that had to mark, thirty years later, the great international wave of author animation, certainly the more important and interesting phenomenon, in terms of quality, in the world history of the sector.

Before dying, Alexeieff entrusted this writer with the collection of reviews that appeared in the press at the time of the first release of *A Night on Bald Mountain*. It was, in his words, the film's pressbook, but also the book concerning the film (the filmmaker loved to play with words, in this case on the double meaning of "book of the press" and "book for the Press"). He gave this collection a meaning of completeness as far as the critical reception of the film had been.

From it we draw here some quotations.

The musicologist and theorist Émile Vuillermoz wrote in *Le Temps* (the date is untraceable):

> Among the new contributions of the film technique, an essay of "animated engraving" made by Alexandre Alexeieff, in an adaptation to the screen of the *Night on Bald Mountain* of Mousorgsky. This is a series of absolutely new effects, whose importance is worth underlining. Responding to a wish that, for my part, I have expressed very often and for a long time, the film directors periodically try to transpose a musical masterpiece onto the screen.
>
> I will not remind my readers of the close ties that unite the grammar and syntax of sentences written for the eye with the grammar and syntax of sentences built for the ear (…) His [Alexeieff's] animated engravings reject every realistic element. Realistic. There are no photographs of reality. Everything here is composition and transposition. But it is not even of the animated drawing in the sense of drawing line that generally applies to this procedure. We are in the presence of a technique of etching, of a subtle vocabulary of nuances, of a range of grays and blacks, of a sort of chalcography or printing, whose patches of light and shadow fade and come to life to infinity. Instead of playing with lines or angles, the artist uses the language of surfaces, volumes and models with changing reliefs. (…) Very rarely I saw a director accepting the disciplines of a score so loyally. Some passages show everything that can be achieved in this field, when you don't want to separate two limbs that are made so well to get along. When the hallucinatory beings holding hands raise and lower their arms, when the music rockets and falls as rain, a musical emotion of the rarest quality is strengthened.

The technique of animated engraving is certainly of great richness and can give the spectators works of the highest interest. In the musical film it has to play a leading role. *A Night on Bald Mountain* is just a first demonstration and a first sampling of this new language. But this film marks a date that we must not forget.

The considerations of Stefan Priacel on the "Spectacles" column of *Regards* magazine (date unknown) follow:

> Two admirable artisans, who are also great artists, Alexandre Alexeieff and Claire Parker, have just made a film, a small film, whose importance however is such that it seems to constitute a date in the history of cinematography. A symphonic work by the great Russian composer Mousorgsky, *A Night on Bald Mountain*, served as a theme for twelve thousand images whose projection lasts just eight minutes. The subject itself of these images does not matter. Let's just say that they are inspired by the fantastic folklore of Ukraine, to which is added the imagination of Alexeieff and Claire Parker. There are witch and demon rides, sabbaths in which dreams are mixed, musicians and birds, horses and fireworks, landscapes that alternate serene and tormented scenes. But the importance of the film is not in the subject, it is in the procedure invented by the two authors, applied here for the first time and whose scope is such that we can say that it is to the cinema what a beautiful painting is to a photograph. Alexandre Alexeieff and Claire Parker call it "animated engraving" (…) It has the extraordinary advantage of offering more than a hundred shades of gray, which is very necessary in film, given the rapidity of the projection.
>
> This fineness of grays allows to pass from one image to another without jerks, through half-tones, giving each

image a complete model. It goes without saying that the human eye is not sensitive enough to distinguish all these nuances, but thanks to this procedure it is possible to create, from one image to another, a transition identical to that of "true photography". (…) Thus it will be possible to make this art which is engraving accessible to a wide public. (…) Alexeieff, one of the most excellent contemporary engravers, is the first to realize this.

Paul Gilson also dwells on the importance of the technical procedure in an article of 18 October 1933 in *L'Intransigeant*. Gilson concludes his paper thus:

> *A Night on Bald Mountain* is the work of two artisans who oppose the conception of work on the assembly line. This work that does not last even half an hour [half an hour, sic] represents more than a year of work. Alexandre Alexeieff and Claire Parker have sometimes lived a second of their film in one day. The witches of *A Night on Bald Mountain* can vanish with the last aquatint of the film: it remains alive as it once was the witch teacher, Itta. The Sabbath of *A Night on Bald Mountain* has the beauty of the devil.

Enthusiastic, finally, is the note that the great British filmmaker, organiser, and producer John Grierson dedicates to the film in *Cinema Quarterly* of autumn 1934:

> This short film introduces a new method of animation, the particulars of which are the secret of the inventor, Alexeieff. The general effect is of animated engraving. There is a soft shadowy quality in the form, and none of the hard precision of line associated with cartoons. The forms emerge from space, they have the appearance of dissolving to other forms. Three dimensional qualities

seem to be easily achieved, and models in animation can be introduced without disturbing the general style. The film, apart of its technical interest, is an imaginative performance, though difficult to describe. Imagine, however, a *Walpurgis Nacht,* in which animated footsteps indicate spirit presence, goblins and hobgoblins appear and disappear and tumble fantastically, scarecrows do a fandango with their shadows on empty hillsides, white horses and black tear across high heaven and skeletons walk. The animation is to the music of Mussorgsky. All films societies should see this film. It is as astonishing and as brilliant a short as they are likely to find.

The readers have probably observed that, while some reviewers scrupulously adhere to the dictates of the opening credits (which reads "Animated engravings of Alexeieff and Claire Parker"), others only mention the man's name. The phenomenon will be repeated in the following decades, so much so that still the name of Claire Parker is relatively little known even to specialists.

This lack has not to do with a male chauvinist bullying (Alexandre always tried to promote Claire's merits), but rather with the mentality of "Making loans only to the rich", which extended to the film the unique signature of the already accredited etcher. Luckily, this time the damage has been limited. According to Claire Parker herself and to unanimous testimony of those who knew their working method, most of the contribution, in the creative field, was due to Alexandre Alexeieff.

# CHAPTER 8

# Dreams of Alexeieff

I T HAS BEEN ARGUED for many decades that people dream in black and white. Today this idea is rejected, but it was common currency at the time of Alexandre Alexeieff and certainly had a basis in the consciousness of the dreaming person. The memory of nocturnal images is blurred, based more on impressions than on images, echoing badly remembered plots – then completed by conscious reinterpretation: a bit like black-and-white cinema, which has evocation characteristics much superior to realistic colour film.

It is therefore no coincidence that Alexeieff, intimately indebted to the dream and to memory for his creation, has always done – when he wanted to make art and not advertising – black-and-white films, and that he has always opposed colour in general, considering it to be ornamental and in fact irrelevant on an aesthetic level. Colour was useful only in making the works "pretty" in the eyes of culturally less well-equipped users. The opinion is personal and certainly not acceptable, but it was rooted in the artist and must be taken into account in thinking about him and his work.

A universe in black and white, then. To which the pinscreen technique attributes blurred contours, such as the images that come to us when we fall asleep; and to which we do not bring all the synaesthesia of our present body, but a sort of selected, eminently emotional and visionary participation. Alexeieff did not believe in art as a reproduction of reality, he did not believe (he often repeated that) in an orchestra's three-dimensionality. He asserted: "I play fiddle". And he built works based on free mental associations, allusions, suggestions, echoes. Like lyric poetry. Like the re-enactment of dreams. He was in good company. Although he was proudly individualistic and pursued an autonomous and unassailable inspiration, he was a frequent visitor to the surrealists, a friend for the whole life of one of them in particular and the most radical: Philippe Soupault.

The passion of the surrealists for the dream is known. When the surveillance of reason has diminished, the constraint of social issues is cancelled. In the dream activity there was no automatic writing through artifices that inhibited the conscience (alcohol, drugs, "cretinising evenings", games like exquisite corpse): the subconscious turned into surreal without translation tools.

American director Henry Hathaway directed *Peter Ibbetson* in 1935. It is the story of a man (Gary Cooper) unjustly condemned to life imprisonment, but who every night, in the misery of his prison, can free himself from the current situation and reunite with the woman he loves (Ann Harding), who dreams the same dream of him. Leaving aside the assessments on quality (not negligible), the film is remembered because the surrealists saw there one of their theoretical cornerstones. (Actually the original text was a novel by George Du Maurier.) For Alexeieff, *Peter Ibbetson* was this and something more. That bond that was retied every night also represented the mirror of an indelible devotion: his for the native Russia he had abandoned, that he could not forget – but it is more accurate to say that he refused to – and that still lived in him at times when vigilance was relaxed.

Sigmund Freud argued that all dreams are the hallucinatory realisation of a desire (Gesammelte Schriften, II, pp. 126–136). If it is allowed to force the reasoning a bit, we could say that the entire artistic/dreaming activity of Alexandre Alexeieff is the hallucinatory realisation of a return to maternal Russia. First in the form of a nightmare with *A Night on Bald Mountain*; the artist himself claimed to have understood, only after many years, that he had described the tragedy of the death of his own father in the fall of the white horse, and the consequent clouding over of his mother in the struggle between the witches. The same approach fits to the fantastic reworking of *The Nose* (from Gogol, 1963). Eventually, we see it as a sentimental and cultural evocation with *Pictures at an Exhibition* (1972) and *Three Moods* (1980).

It would be an error of perspective to consider Alexeieff as the last of the romantics, and to read his work, both cinematographic and illustrational, as a collection of sighs dedicated to the things, to the people and to the places he desired. Other components were also very incisive in him, from the experimental to the humorous to the exotic. Even the perpetual resumption of the thread of the discourse on Russia was much more reasoned and articulated than a simple devotion to the birthplace: he had a very high literary admiration towards *Doctor Zhivago*, of which he left us a splendid illustrated edition. The admiration for Solgenitsin's prose was also very high; his mindset and personal history as a political opponent (in which he could have found a reflection of himself) did not touch him on the contrary for nothing.

One could essentially say that in this author (so different yet always so identical, so elusive yet so powerful) the memory is an ethical choice, therefore pre-aesthetic and of connotative consequence of the whole work. "I am a conservative", he observed in a letter addressed to this writer, "but not in the political sense: rather in the sense that I would never want the things that really have value lost".

The selection of things that really had value (even pictorial, even cinematographic) was by Alexeieff made a priori with respect to the material creation of images; and from this mental warehouse the scene to be reproduced was then extracted from time to time.

In *Pictures from an Exhibition* and in *Three Moods* we see land-scapes from childhood, corners of the maternal house, domestic furniture, toys, and the comrades of the Petersburg cadet school in which he himself studied.

In his life Alexeieff only once made a copy from life: when he asked his wife, Claire Parker, to pose for the etchings dedicated to the *Man's Fate* of Malraux. It was for the portrait of a dead woman and he always said, laughing and almost apologetically, that he needed his most lively affection to be able to trace the mourning with a sure hand.

# CHAPTER 9

# Bruno Bozzetto*

*His Early Years*

B RUNO BOZZETTO BEGAN HIS artistic career in 1958 with *Tapum! The History of Weapons*. He was only twenty years old, and for four years he had been making narrow gauge films, learning and experimenting with animation techniques on his own. The film is admired everywhere, receives awards (in Mulhouse and Rapallo), and is favourably reviewed. In the traditionally poor panorama of Italian animated films, the name of the young Milanese became an obligatory point of reference from the first moment.

The second part of the 1950s is perhaps the most tumultuous period of Italian animation. Once the stammering of the pioneering generation had ended, and the attempts at full-length films had failed (*La rosa di Bagdad* by Domeneghini and *The Dynamite Brothers* by Pagot, both from 1949), the activity turned to theatrical advertising. The area was not vast, but the chance of survival was assured.

---

\* Originally published as a booklet with the title *Animazione primo amore* (*My First Love, Animation*, Milan: ISCA, 1972). Updated and revised version.

The novelty year was 1957 when the state broadcaster RAI opened its one television channel to advertising. The prime-time program was called *Carosello*, and it was a series of installments, each one combining an entertainment "body" and a "pigtail" dedicated to praising the product. The small screen suddenly expanded the market, while the nascent economic boom skyrocketed the demand for audiovisual advertising. Many small producers found new sap, others were born and entered the lists; the ongoing activity refined the technique of the animators, and the best ones abandoned the companies in which they had carried out their apprenticeship to set up on their own.

Bruno Bozzetto made his encounter with advertising in 1960, after another two years as an amateur. In the process of selling equipment and dedicating himself to university exams, he came across an old friend one day. He sees his work and gives him an order for the company of which he is an emissary. It is the birth of the first, very short advertising series: five episodes, based on the character of Kuko.

From this moment the activity of the "Bruno Bozzetto Film" would be split into two channels of advertising and entertainment films, in a kind of mutualistic symbiosis whereby the former finances the latter and the latter acts as promotion for the former.

It was indispensable, to keep faith with these intentions, to create an agile structure. Bozzetto needed a team: his goals were too industrial for him to work alone and too creative for an impersonal organisation like that of the American and Japanese studios of the time to be tolerated.

He manages to bring together a good number of intelligent, young and enthusiastic collaborators; with them he decides to attempt the feat that for sixteen years has disturbed the sleep of Italian animators, captivating them and rejecting them: the feature film.

In 1965 *West and Soda* premiered at the "Arlecchino" cinema in Milan. The public flows in large numbers, even if an unpredictable fact dampens the interest: during the slow processing of the animated film, Sergio Leone has made *Per un pugno di dollari* (*A Fistful of Dollars*) and uncorked the phenomenon of the Spaghetti western, obviously in competition with Bozzetto's film. However, the result is positive. The team proves to be valid. Ermanno Comuzio extends a nice compliment to the twenty-seven-year-old author writing:

> Bozzetto seems to be the one who sums up all the Italian animation filmmakers, fusing in his company – more workshop in the Renaissance sense than industrial studio – art and technique, that is the taste and the ability to create, to experiment, to propose a style, with the indispensable instrumental needs of an efficient organism.[1]

*West and Soda* taught an inattentive and unaware audience that animators existed and operated in Italy, capable of producing a film on the level of Hollywood productions. The next *VIP, My Brother Superman* had the favour of the public as well, but in the meantime, through the breach opened by Bozzetto, more people had passed to feature film (the Gavioli brothers, Zac, the Cenci brothers).

Some commentators claim that these are the least beautiful works coming from the Via Melchiorre Gioia atelier in Milan. Maybe. The same could be valid for TV opening titles, like the fortunate "Donna Rosa" of the *Settevoci* show, to which another considerable part of the notoriety of the studio is linked. However, these were the only means of engaging the public in animation. A difficult courtship, which pushes the author of animated films to make concessions to the current taste to the detriment of the genuineness of his own inspiration and the linguistic characteristics of the medium (the concise character of the animated expression is not suitable for the length of the feature film).

After *VIP* Bozzetto experienced a period of crisis, which lasts two years and during which he makes only two short films (but

*Ego* belongs more to the background designer Mulazzani than to him). He comes out of the black-dog period abandoning the unloved advertising activity and devoting himself instead of making his "personal" films.

Bozzetto gives a precise indication in the humanistic direction, openly pronouncing himself for the artistic characteristics of animation as a craft. "If I have to go to the assembly line and sell a product, then I'd rather produce something else. Shoes, for example, why not".[2]

## MR. ROSSI

Before 1960, the year of *An Oscar for Mr. Rossi*, Bozzetto had populated his films with bizarre figurines for the sole purpose of enriching the plot, which was the real reason of interest. Mr. Rossi, on the other hand, sacrifices the narrative structure of the film. Bozzetto's love for his creature will remain alive for decades, demonstrating how a figure born almost by chance was able to objectify the author's world well.

Mr. Rossi is enough a character as to primarily attract the interest of the viewer and make the plot pass in the second line. However, his personality, once delineated, never deepens, remains in a state of hint. Many might prefer the contemptuous diction of "caricature" and decide that a character without psychology is a failure without remedy.

This writer thinks that Mr. Rossi is a close relative of the Chaplinian tramp, of the Buster Keatonian great stone face, of the young-man-with-horn-rimmed-glasses of Harold Lloyd. In the great and fruitful tradition of the American vaudeville of 1910–1920, the animated short film by Terry and Fleischer and Disney finds its roots; from these, in turn, the Italian-drawn comedian is born, although contaminated with the great lesson of the United Productions of America (UPA) and above all of Bobe Cannon (see the stylistic analogies with *Gerald McBoing Boing*, 1951).

Bozzetto's comedy is rooted in the principles and recipes of the Californian one reel, although filtered through a European vision (with the eye more to the intellect than to the instinct, and therefore blander in the rhythms of the action), and although restrained in the graphic sign (the "I style" of the UPA against the round opulence of the "O style" of Disney): the chase (*Mr. Rossi Buys a Car*), the gag (classically formed by premise, expectation, surprise; see the episode of the bather in *Mr. Rossi to the Beach*), the absurd (the examples are multiple; think to the seller of *An Oscar for Mr. Rossi* whose face turns into a record player while he repeats his rigmarole always the same). The French scholar Jean-Pierre Coursodon, in synthesising the definition of a vaudevillian hero, provides a portrait that fits perfectly with our Rossi: "A handicapped man, who is saved from annihilation only thanks incessant stratagems typical of the oppressed, and thanks to a paradoxically enormous luck".[3]

After what has been said, it is clear why the character should not be investigated with psychological tools, which do not belong to him. Hero of vaudeville, it fulfils the task of all vaudeville heroes: it acts.

Lloyd's horn-rimmed-glasses man had rudimentary features, which indicated him as the dreamer but full of energy and practical optimism. Chaplin was the eternal dispossessed, Langdon the teenager, Keaton was so many things, perhaps all coming from the moon.

These summary and – above all – generic characteristics constituted the viaticum for which the viewer who considered himself an adolescent, or disinherited, or petty bourgeois, could identify himself in the hero and laugh with gusto at the comic aspects of his daily life; at the variations on the theme that happened to his avatar on the screen.

The secret, for the actor, was then to identify the "type" for which he felt he was cut, and then identify the actions, the facts, the experiences that were to the "type", as well as congenial and habitual. Afterward, it was only a question of turning them to ridicule. The merits of the American comedy arise from these foundations of structure; and they are the inexhaustible fantasy, the inventive genius, the acumen of observation, the mastery in orchestrating the effects. The satire of custom is lacking, and those who seek it at all costs (there have been, and there are) are guilty of cultural provincialism.

Bozzetto's man in the street is the portrait of a hot-tempered petty bourgeois, ugly and uptight because he is unable to excel in anything. A victim, almost always, of events that are everyday stuff but which turn out to be bigger than him (and, it seems appropriate to say, only him, which frustrates him even more), but he is always ready to try again. He is eternally in the quest of an ideal: that may be a hit (*Rossi Oscar*), tranquillity (*Rossi Beach*, *Rossi Campsite*), leisure (*Rossi Skiing, Rossi Safari*), or the desire to keep up with the times (*Rossi Car*).

The classic structure of his adventures sees a beginning, in which Rossi forms this ideal (or by dreaming, or by casually encountering it); a development, which summarises the troubles on which he bangs his head; and an ending, mostly bitter, that records his failure.

In Rossi, the viewer can identify himself, laugh at his own tics, at his own faults. There is always a certain underlying flattery alive (also ancient as the school of comedy in entertainment).

In other words, the character is too wretched to allow complete identification by the viewer. As far as satire is concerned, this is the limit of Bruno Bozzetto's satire. The type of people whom he sees in real life – and then puts on the screen – can laugh at things that no one refuses to laugh at. He will not be shamed for what he should not want to discuss publicly or for what "is no joke".

These considerations do not entail a value judgement. Every author has his own poetic world and his own ideology, and no one will want to expect from Bozzetto what Bozzetto was not born to give. We have clarified the features of his satire precisely to avoid the risk of elevating to an aesthetic criterion that it is the ferocity or yielding of the invective.

## THE FEATURE FILM

For the general public, "film" is synonymous with "feature film". The approach with such a general public then passes through the Caudine Forks of the hour and a half of projection; then if we talk about animation, here is another drain: "animation" means "Disney", and "animated film" means "cinematic fable for children". (It follows that if a work is for children, it is not suitable for refined adults; consequently, it is not appropriate to disturb the aesthetics.)

Here's the crossroads: Compete with Disney by putting yourself on the same level, giving the public what they already want, or compete with Disney by denying it and trying to attract the public with a novelty? The first way leads to financial and artistic failure, the second is no less risky, but at least it allows the author to keep faith with his/her inspiration.

*West and Soda* and *VIP, My Brother Superman* are expressions of the second way of trying luck. Both imperfect for some commercial compromises, especially the second; but recognisably signed Bozzetto in every sequence. Both possess intelligence, vivacity, and sarcasm, in a dose that perhaps frightens some parents in search of harmless fables, but definitely have qualities for those who approach show business-land with a receptive mind.

We are facing two parodies: the parody of the western in *West and Soda*, complete with a neurotic gunslinger, a girl called Clementine (think of the namesake song), a very bad boss, redskins, and bluejackets; and a parody of the adventure comic books in *VIP*. It is a way always known to comedy if it is true that Aristophanes parodied Euripides; and that fits well with the spirit of our filmmaker, made of acute observation and propensity to demystifying laughter.

Tradition serves as a connective; using it as a support, Bozzetto can work at ease, not constrained by narrative or explanation commitments. Proceeding with another directive, we arrive at the same result. The paramount recipe of the vaudeville farce consists of choosing a physical environment as a theme, from which to draw all the possible inventions (those who know, for instance, Stan Laurel, know what incredible variations on the theme he can draw from a door that does not close). A step further, and we are at the choice of a tradition, well known to the public as a physical environment and to the exploitation of all the opportunities it offers. The parody, therefore, serves to sketch the circle.

The feature film implies narrativity, thinking in prose. The greats of the golden age of comedy had to radically transform their works when they passed from the two reels to the hour and a half of projection. In the beginning, an idea was enough, a skeleton whose pulp would have been the gags; then it was necessary to create psychologies, plots, secondary actions. In short, to embark into screwball comedy.

This way of entertaining audiences is difficult to reach, with a medium like the animated cartoon. This does not allow psychological investigations and mimic games; its linguistic features are conciseness and non-narrativity. The point is, therefore, to dilute as long as it is possible the characteristics of the short film and arrive at last at the fateful running time. Dress a large body in a tight dress, make the circle square.

Bozzetto manages quite well in the intent, in the one case as in the other. *West and Soda* is not boring; it does not suffer from showy slowdowns; it is rich in brilliant gags and acute details. At least two sequences are textbook: the aggression of the ants to Johnny, and the final duel between the hero and Despicable. The best of the film, however, lies in even more minute touches. Here are some: a completely original absurdity (the cows that open up like refrigerators, the horse equipped with a speedometer, the devil who emerges from the ground to take Despicable); and some minor characters (Socrates the drunkard dog, the two gravediggers, the moose head in the house of Despicable). On the other hand, three aggressions and violence at Clementine's house are frankly too many; the elements of gold and land tenure end up overlapping and performing the same function of pushing Despicable against the two positive heroes.

Nor Clementine herself, Ursus, Slim, or Esmeralda are satisfactorily fully expressed. Dominant is Despicable, half Shylock and half Al Capone, and also the figure of Johnny, the gunslinger in a crisis of conscience and with the Stetson eternally lowered on the face (he takes it off only once, on the diligence, and for a few tenths of a second; this writer has seen the film in slow motion and can testify that he has brown hair and a parting).

*VIP, My Brother Superman* had an arduous production. At first, it had to parody the adventures of The Phantom; the little Vip had to be the hero's caricature (the elements of the aquiline nose and the red costume remained); Happy Betty had to be Neapolitan and even have a boyfriend. American capital intervened, so there was a reorganisation from which the handsome SuperVip was born, then Nervustrella, Lisa, and the little songs to fill downtime. American capital volatilised.

Despite these accidents, the filigree of the film remains good, and the praises made about the previous one could be repeated. The differentiating element consists of greater thematic maturity and a broader intellectual commitment, where the former was above all characterised by imagination and youthful enthusiasm (even the dominant colours are warm in one and cold in the other).

Particularly interesting is the insert on advertising and mass communication. An insert that is perhaps disharmonious and too long, but very much in line with the underlying spirit.

The two VIPs represent the champions of human nature against massification, and massification is not the usual future danger that in dystopic narratives is vanquished in the name of the "good" present. It is precisely our present, which the island of Happy Betty portrays in perfect miniature. The scientist who carries out the demonstration would not dream of being confident on the condition of the human brain of today: his problem is to use the brain missile for good rather than for evil. To let the mind reboot itself is just not an option.

The visit that Happy Betty makes her shareholders perform through the factory gives the dismay. Midgets all the same work under a heavy yoke, and for their "holidays" they are canned in long afferent tubes (our highways?) and conveyed to places of leisure no less false and neurotic than the world they have left. Only the voice-over comment, of light humour, mitigates the impression that leaves this concentration camp world. Hope, the author seems to tell us, lies in the simple man, in the concrete conscience of each of us. The one who removes chestnuts from the fire is not the invincible giant, but the small Vip, the one who is kicked and punched, is short-sighted, and flutters for a few metres panting for fatigue. Bozzetto's humanistic spirit manifests itself in full: when the measure of man is lost, it is up to him to regain it, without hoping for anything from superheroes or semi-magical equivalents.

## SHORT FILMS

*Alpha Omega* dates back to 1961. A schematic character, in a static shot, lives his parable from birth to death, from alpha to omega. The various enticements and the various opportunities of existence are presented to him, in the form of brief appearances: education, love, goodness, marriage, work, health. When he is close to dying, he calls the poor to whom he had not given a coin, frees the bird he had caged. The film has a slow, moving trend, in which even the smiling notes give more tenderness than joy.

The theme of man's destiny returns, much more mature and motivated, in *A Life in a Box*, which is from 1967. Here the contrast between the world of fantasy and beauty is symbolised by the vision of a very colourful nature and by a piece of music that evokes joy, and the dehumanising contemporary world. The beginning is a subtly allegoric trompe l'oeil (what appears to be a rising sun is the belly of a pregnant woman dressed in red).

Nothing in this film could be added or removed; as a whole, it is a small jewel of cinematographic poetry. The timing, the graphic and sound solutions, everything is fitting and well resolved.

In the same year, 1967, Bozzetto made the third of what we could call lyric films.

"The man and his world" was the theme that the Montreal Expo had proposed to animators around the world, to be held within the fixed duration of one minute. Bozzetto won a silver medal telling of a politician (whose face changes very quickly: Truman, Stalin, Khrushchev, Nasser, and so on) who, while speaking in public, tries to chase away a butterfly that disturbs him. At this point, an increasingly dizzying zooming backwards begins, from the speaker to the earth, to the stars, to the galaxies, until we discover that the galaxies are only a part of the body of another butterfly, similar to the first, which twirls twice and then disappears from the field. The relativity of what surrounds us, the sweetness of nature, the fallibility of man, are underlined by an excellent soundtrack.

Bozzetto's lyrical style is somewhat reminiscent of Guido Gozzano, also due to the image of the butterfly (the Turin writer died before concluding an entomological poem). In both, there is a mixture of emotion and irony, of guarded tenderness, of feeling tempered by scepticism. We should not push the parallel beyond the indication of an analogy, but it testifies how we can compare certain cinema to poetry, without blushing. *I due castelli* (*The Two Castles*, 1963) records the actions of one of two castellans who tries to storm the manor facing it. The tidy drawing and the originality of the gags (some of which will be reproduced in *West and Soda*) constitute the titles of merit of this work.

*I due castelli* is bare and linear; *Ego* (1969) instead is leafy and colourful. The structure of the dream, that is two thirds of the film, is based on an evocative technique that is often too subtle to be communicative. Although it shines in many points of intelligence, the film seems to be among the least personal (after all, the hand of the scenographer Giovanni Mulazzani is present perhaps more than that of Bozzetto himself), and the presence of horror elements, like the long lines of hanged people, seems to confirm it.

*Sottaceti* (*Pickles*, 1971) is a series of film-pill each of which portrays a concept: war, hunger, religion, et cetera.

The taste of the brief apologue, of the pregnant gimmick, has always been alive in this author who claims his highest admiration for the Japanese Yoji Kuri and his short and cruel animated flashes. In *Pickles*, the expressive maturity is achieved, as well as the disappearance of the juvenile residues, at both thematic and expressive levels.

The *Conquests* sequence shows the mountain so painfully climbed collapse on the two climbers. The composition of the titles of each chapter is rhythmic and spectacular (sometimes the letters make the whims), and if the drawing is less polished than usual (Bozzetto has drawn and coloured by himself here), it is more expressive.

## BEFORE THE BEGINNING

The first animation work of the man who would have been nicknamed "The Italian Disney" has to do with Disney: it's a Donald Duck cartoon. Shot in black and white, 8 mm, the film dates back to 1953 and is no more than a technical experiment. A roughly drawn Donald Duck walks (on a background that wobbles, because it was redesigned every time; no cels then) until he comes across a newspaper in the ground whose title reads: "The Martians are coming". Donald catches a sign with the sentence "Then we flee" and vanishes. This first approach would just be a curiosity if there was not a notable element: that zoom towards the newspaper headline that could not be done "in the camera" and that therefore had to be drawn every time by hand. A precise stylistic choice, already tenaciously pursued (to save the effort it would have been enough to proceed by straight cut), demonstrating the good stuff of the fifteen-year-old author.

*Indian Fantasy* (8 mm black and white, 1954) shows that the first lesson was useful. The rhythm is well directed by the filmmaker; the first gags make their appearance; we note the use of some cels.

In 1955 Bozzetto tried to animate puppets. It had to be a science fiction movie, with small robots and shining spaceships. It was not completed, and only a few outtakes remain. At the same time, Bozzetto tried his hand at live action. Of 1954 is *I ladri che mascalzoni* (*Thieves, What Rogues!*), based on a chase (the fugitive is a thief specialised in disguises) and made sapid by some film tricks. *Il cerchio si stringe* (*The Circle Tightens*) of the same year seems the continuation of the previous one (characterized by pursuits and camouflages that follow one another on the roofs of Milan).

These amateur films, such as the following and unfinished *Due ragni nel piatto* (*Two Spiders on the Plate*, 1958), are the anticipation of the lifelong taste for the slapstick film with actors, with camouflages and sneers of the comedian who hunt him down.

Equally significant are the documentaries on nature (*Piccolo mondo amico* [*Little World Friend*], 1955; *I gatti che furbacchioni* [*The Smartass Cats*], 1956; *Sul filo dell'erba* [*On a Thread of Grass*], 1957; *Il solito documentario* [*The Usual Documentary*], 1959).

They testify to Bruno Bozzetto's love of nature, a love that we find in the entire subsequent work, and which is also expressed in the recurring interest for insects (see the humorous book *Thousand Little Cretins*). Secondly, they prove how rooted was the graphic choice of the "very small", which we will find throughout his career (think of how many ants, or people in long shot, he has staged). Finally, the documentaries represent a further tutorial on Disney, this time the one of the series *The True-Life Adventures*. In this case, Bozzetto accepts the Disney principle of the documentary show, that is of his non-scientific nature. However, he deliberately chooses not to go into the "beautiful image", in the formal game, and to keep his style sober and close to the subject.

Last I left *Tico-Tico* and *Partita a dama* (*Game of Checkers*; both dated 1959–1960). They are already mature, as evidenced by the production date itself, following that of the often -mentioned *Tapum!*

On the rhythm of the famous Brazilian samba, *Tico-Tico* unfolds a series of semi-abstract metamorphoses, engraved on black film in the manner of Norman McLaren. At that time Bozzetto had for the first time seen the Scot/Canadian animator's films and had then had the opportunity to meet him. If it is true that *Tico-Tico* resembles *Blinkity-Blank*, it is equally true that no careful eye would miss the distance between one and the other. Nor is it only a question of technical mastery: the film of the Montreal genius is all about abstract rhythms, a challenge to human intellect, research, and evocation; while that of the young Milanese is joyful and sparkling and is anchored to the immediate intelligibility of what takes place on the screen. Equally McLaren-inspired is *Game of Checkers*, which makes use of the *Rythmetic* lesson. The pawns play the game by themselves, and during the performance they have a chance to quarrel among themselves, to show shyness or stubbornness. The theme will be resumed, albeit from a different angle, in one of *Pickles*'s fragments.

McLaren's influence will always remain latent and never manifest. It could be said that McLaren was a master of synthesis, of self-control, of dry expression; that is, that he was a much more fruitful and useful teacher than is usually the case for the stylistic and thematic models that young people choose.

## THE MOUSE, THE DUCK, AND THE STRIP

Outside the borders of Italy, Mickey and Donald & Co. comic strips or books have been received very mildly, and the names of Floyd Gottfredson (Mickey) and Carl Barks (Donald) are far from being a legend. In Italy, they reigned for almost seventy years, and they also provided suggestions for Bruno Bozzetto's first films. Here are some examples. Mr. Rossi, standing on the ski lift, freezes into an ice cube (*Rossi sci*); the same, after having shattered and recomposed the camera several times, repairs it "definitively", and doesn't care of surplus pieces (*Rossi Oscar*); the scientist is segregated, and fed with bones, by the powerful who wants him at his/her services (*VIP*). In other words, the Milanese author was able to learn and reuse material from his predecessors, despite having much to create.

According to the ancient recipe, a gag consists of a dynamic structure, in which a certain fact produces a development that appears consistent and reasonable; then a twist, a "surprise" follows this development. The latter interrupts the logical trend, lets the irrational flow suddenly, and thereby generates laughter.

To us, it seems interesting that the gag mixes with emotion, the one to which Bozzetto above all points ("For me, the gag is: a surprise plus a concept").

The emotional gag is not new (Chaplin used it, and Keaton used it); but Bozzetto was able to command it with full mastery (think, for example, of that collection of gags that is *Pickles*). Some attention should instead be given to the "sound" element. The spoken word has little space. With the exception of narrative feature films, Bozzetto utilises allusive sound, vocal distortions, and synthetic effects. A cinema that makes its flag of synthesis and significance cannot be linked to the logical threads of prose.

These "special" sounds integrate the image; they are its continuation in another language. The same cannot always be said about music, even if it structurally carries out the same function as the sound effects. The music of *A Life in a Box* is skilfully appropriate, while that of *Mr. Rossi at the Sea* just doesn't work.

It is no discovery that verbal humour is very different from the visual one. One can exist when the other is absent: and so, *VIP*'s long excursus on the evils of mass communication is verbal humour, grafted onto visual support that is almost documentary.

## CULTURED, NOT NEEDING BOOKS

Mr. Rossi's cinematic adventure dealing with the Oscar is a well-thought-out entertainment film: and it is also an acute satire of certain festivals and fashions. For the author, the latent danger is the uncontrolled joke: in two words, moral indifference. Only a solid culture can constitute a bulwark: meaning a sure taste, a solid ideology, a constant breadth of views. Bozzetto's constant control over his creative material is obvious. Everything in him seems spontaneous, his good taste seems innate, not a shade of a built, bookish culture. Despite the very long cinematographic militia, his works preserve that enthusiasm and the naïveté typical of the neophyte. It seems to me beautiful – because incisive – the definition that his colleague Max Massimino-Garniér once gave of him: "A cultured man without books".

The vision of the world, and the tools to interpret and recreate it, come to him from the experience of every day and from his personal history, rather than from erudition. An only child (therefore often alone) of wealthy parents, he shows in his work some classical constants of the bourgeois artist: interest in the problems of the individual (rather than of society), anxiety about the destiny of man on earth, the longing for a more natural state than the one in which he lives. The years of childhood passed not far from the ski fields and the summer hills have induced in the artist's spirit an incurable antithesis between the world he has known and loved, and the acrid world in which he operates today. The "social" part of Bozzetto's irony is exhausted in this. He scratches on the surface, mocks the symptoms instead of the disease; its controversy does not reach the root of the phenomenon and the identification of a buggy society, but it stops at the condemnation of the facts. Some may grieve and blame him. But such an attitude would mean not understanding the characteristics of our director, who presents himself as a sensitive witness of the tensions present in his time and of those that are arriving. The non-triviality, the non-contingency of Bozzetto's art are witnessed by the fact that the older works are still thematically vibrant. But that he is neither a sociologist nor a political scientist nor even a philosopher, is witnessed by the same caution of his polemic, which avoids proposing an alternative to the evils he deciphers. The alternative will have to come from the awakening of the viewer's conscience; and with this Bozzetto will have exhausted his task, as it was for – say – the South African William Kentridge (who had to do with apartheid).

Since his early years, Bozzetto seems to have a precise awareness of his function as an artist, his ideas and lucidity would become even stronger than at the beginning. In 1976, he will sign his long-length masterpiece: *Allegro Non Troppo*.

## NOTES

1. Ermanno Comuzio, "Piccola storia del disegno animato italiano", in *Cineforum* 53, March 1966, p. 235, Bergamo.
2. Personal communication with Giannalberto Bendazzi, 1970.
3. Jean-Pierre Coursodon, *Keaton & Cie – Les burlesques américains du «muet»*, Paris: Seghers, 1964, p. 53.

# CHAPTER 10

# Address

## *Rossi, Mitteleuropa*

I REMEMBER A LESSON I was given when I was a young critic on my debut. I was attending the preview of Franco Giraldi's film *Solitary Hearts*, starring Ugo Tognazzi and Senta Berger. At the end of the screening, I commented that Berger's performance seemed particularly good to me, especially considering that she, an Austrian with a Hollywood past, had impersonated a woman of the Lombard bourgeoisie, therefore a figure far removed from her direct experiences. Giraldi replied to me, a little paternal and somewhat ironic: "Look, it was an easy figure. It is the bourgeoisie of Mitteleuropa. In Vienna, she grew up among women of that type". Giraldi was from Trieste, Mitteleuropean par excellence.

It is my thesis that there is a bourgeois population of central Europe and that Italian animation is not wrong to believe that its Mr. Rossi is understandable and captivating even beyond Brenner to the north and beyond Opicina to the east.

This moustachioed, short-haired, red-dressed character, always a victim of frustration and small mishaps, was the protagonist of several short films, comics on TV, comic books, and some television series in the 1960s and 1970s. He was born in

1960, when a short of the twenty-two-year-old Bruno Bozzetto was rejected from the festival of his family's city, Bergamo. As a "poet's revenge", Bozzetto designed the caricature of the director of that event, and around the cartoon he built the sarcastic story of an amateur filmmaker who is first despised and then accidentally honoured (*An Oscar for Mr. Rossi*).

The saga of Rossi can be read in various ways, but the first that comes to mind is that of a drawn version of the successful "Comedy the Italian way". Like Sordi, Manfredi, Tognazzi, and Villaggio, the grotesque protagonists, our hero is also a middle-man; to the point that his name itself is the most widespread in the country. He is a cheap, mediocre, frustrated loser who either endures failures or consoles himself with imagination.

It is certainly not a new figure: its origins date back to the theatre piece Monssù Travet (1863), born from playwright Vittorio Bersezio's pen. But it has a specific culture behind it. Heir of the free enterprise and capitalism that has flourished in the Po Valley for a thousand years, Rossi is far from self-pity, from fatalism, from the narcissistic self-injury of Roman films. To adversity he reacts trying to assert his reasons; he perseveres and tries again instead of "getting by"; he rejects compromises. It is not surprising that Hungarian animation gave birth to his artistic brother, Gusztav. Today I know that for two centuries the political and social consonances between Northern Italy and Hungary have been innumerable, so much so that even among the Garibaldi's Thousand there were three Magyars.

Rossi has changed over time as times have changed. At first, he was a trifling thing struggling with the dreams of the 1960s: making the "little film", going to the mountains and the sea, buying a car. Later, he travelled to Venice and Africa. In the 1970s we see him engaged in affairs as an opulent businessman, with a house outside the city and a doghouse-keeper.

Then came the 1980s, 1990s, and 2000s. Probably the anti-heroic hero had its day in the advanced society of the whole world.

Animation no longer has Mickey Mouse, Bugs Bunny, Daffy Duck, and Tom and Jerry, that a few decades ago gave birth to a small but vibrant epic of the everyday life reinterpreted through zoomorphic figures.

In the 2000s and 2010s, the film characters have been of pure fantasy; reality has no grip on the public. The average citizen goes instead to the supermarket of culture, as it goes to that of food, vacation, or information. Buy and consume.

Pessimist? Not at all. Mr. Rossi and his colleagues from trans-alpine and Danuban adventures are even more important than yesterday. They are a historical document, the digital imprint of what we will call the Cold War Society. A season which is the mother of that of the new century, and still must be analysed; and that in addition to economic and political teachings, also has many ethical teachings to deliver to us. It may not have been better than the one that lived in the first half of the twentieth century and that faced dictatorships, invasions, and military conflicts. But it knew how to evolve, also and perhaps precisely because he knew how to look at itself; not infrequently with the right irony.

# CHAPTER 11

# The Egg of Cohl

*F*ANTASMAGORIE, CONCEIVED, DESIGNED, AND directed by Parisian Émile Cohl in 1908, is considered by many to be the first animated film in history, and by all still a classic. For the duration of two and a half minutes, Cohl puts on characters quickly sketched, intent on being metamorphosed and playing tricks.

The non-plot plot seems to be kneaded by a surrealist in the mood for automatic writing, but in fact it is rather the umpteenth appearance of that karst river which is the art of the absurd, and which is as old as the human intellect. We see a hand drawing a small character, white on a black background. They disappear behind a man who falls from above and then sits in a movie theatre. Disturbed by the big lady's hat that occupies the seat in front of him, he tears off the feathers of the hat one by one.

From the lady's lorgnette glasses reappears the first character, who absorbs the man, then interacts with a soldier, a bottle, an elephant, a house; climbs to the first floor and from there falls materially losing its head in the impact with the pavement. The hand returns to the scene and recomposes the body, which swells like a balloon, mounts on a horse, and finally gallops away on the latter.

*Fantasmagorie* is one of the most viewed films in the world, first in festivals, retrospectives, and special evenings, and now on YouTube. In 2017, in the imminence of the nineteenth convention of the Society for Animation Studies (Padova, 3–7 July), I was lazily watching it on my PC.

I realised that I was seeing something new.

In the scene set in the movie theatre we were faced with a film in the film; to a *mise en abîme*, to put it in critical jargon. While the character performs the main action by removing the feathers from the lady's hat, a movie starring drawn characters passes on the screen (the screen of the room in which the action takes place). The curtain falls and rises again on abstract animated drawings.

The message is important. In this way Cohl claimed an industrial future for the medium he was creating, and foresaw the birth and success of abstract animation.

Keep in mind that in 1908 abstract animation did not exist yet, and that abstract painting itself would become fashionable only a couple of years later, with Vasily Kandinsky. It seemed to me unlikely that I would be the first, after a century or so of projections, to notice this elementary sleight of hand (focus attention on one main action and send the message through the secondary action). I sifted through the books and accessible articles on Émile Cohl. Donald Crafton[1] was the only one to describe the scene, but he didn't dwell on the meaning.

I made public this discovery with a communication at the conference in Padua, sitting at the table of speakers together with Donald Crafton. He supplemented the information, adding that the copies visible today are drawn by a single English copy found decades ago. It was probably of a larger size, so the sides had been cut in the 35 mm transfer. Here is the possible reason of the incomplete visibility of the drawn screen, otherwise unexplainable.

It is said (notice: it is pure historical invention) that Christopher Columbus would one day talk with some dignitaries of the court of Spain, and that these would diminish his enterprise by claiming that, by all accounts, anyone would have been able to do it. In response, he challenged them in another endeavour: to keep a hard-boiled egg standing on the table. Each made numerous attempts, but none succeeded. They asked Columbus to demonstrate how to solve the case. He made a slight dent at the end of the egg, tapping it lightly against the table. The egg remained straight. When the onlookers protested saying that they could do the same, Columbus replied: "The solution was before your eyes, but you didn't see it".

Our mind constantly tends to give a meaning to reality, selecting among all the stimuli those that are composed in a coherent presupposed image. This tendency entails a consequence: the particular image that the eye and the mind select ends up excluding all other possible images. If this is true, our eyes and our minds have seen the main action for 109 years, excluding the secondary one.

Consequently, I propose to name this case of hidden message in plain sight as "the egg of Cohl".

## NOTE

1. Donald Crafton, *Emile Cohl, Caricature and Film*, Princeton, NJ: Princeton University Press, 1990.

# Index

Note: Page numbers followed by "n" refer to notes.